D1250299

Information Technology Project Management Interview Questions: IT Project Management and Project Management Interview Questions, Answers, and Explanations

Compiled By: Terry Sanchez-Clark

Information Technology Project Management Interview Questions: IT Project Management and Project Management Interview Questions, Answers, and Explanations

ISBN 13: 978-1-933804-74-3

The programs in this book have been included for instructional value only. They have been tested with care but are not guaranteed for any particular purpose.

The publisher does not offer any warranties or representations not does it accept any liabilities with respect to the programs.

Trademarks: All trademarks are the property of their respective owners. Equity Press and ITCOOKBOOK is not associated with any product or vender mentioned in this book.

Printed in the United States of America

Please visit our website at www.itcookbook.com

TABLE OF CONTENTS

INTRODUCTION

A. What is IT Project Management?

(As defined in Wikipedia)

Project management is the discipline of organizing and managing resources in such a way that these resources deliver all the work required to complete a project within defined scope, time, and cost constraints. A project is a temporary and one-time endeavor undertaken to create a unique product or service. This property of being a temporary and a one-time undertaking contrasts with processes, or operations, which are permanent or semi-permanent ongoing functional work to create the same product or service over-and-over again. The management of these two systems is often very different and requires varying technical skills and philosophy, hence requiring the development of project management.

The first challenge of project management is ensuring that a project is delivered within the defined constraints. The second, more ambitious, challenge is the optimized allocation and integration of the inputs needed to meet those pre-defined objectives. The project, therefore, is a carefully selected set of activities chosen to use resources (time, money, people, materials, energy, space, provisions, communication, quality, risk, etc.) to meet the pre-defined objectives.

History of project management
Project management was not used as an isolated concept before the Sputnik crisis of the Cold War. After this crisis, the United States Department of Defense needed to speed up the military project process and new tools (models) for

achieving this goal were invented. In 1958 they invented the Program Evaluation and Review Technique or PERT, as part of the Polaris missile submarine program. At the same time, the DuPont corporation invented a similar model called CPM, critical path method. PERT was later extended with a work breakdown structure or WBS. The process flow and structure of the military undertakings quickly spread into many private enterprises.

There are a number of guiding techniques that have been developed over the years that can be used to formally specify exactly how the project will be managed. These include the Project Management Body of Knowledge (PMBOK), and such ideas as the Personal Software Process (PSP), and the Team Software Process (TSP) and PRINCE2. These techniques attempt to standardize the practices of the development team making them easier to predict and manage as well as track.

Critical chain is the latest extension to the traditional critical path method.

In critical studies of project management, it has been noted that several of these fundamentally PERT-based models are not well suited for the multi-project company environment of today. Most of them are aimed at very large-scale, one-time, non-routine projects, and nowadays all kinds of management are expressed in terms of projects. Using complex models for "projects" (or rather "tasks") spanning a few weeks has been proven to cause unnecessary costs and low maneuverability in several cases. Instead project management experts try to identify different "lightweight" models, such as, for example Extreme Programming for software development and Scrum techniques. The generalization of extreme programming to other kinds of projects is extreme project management, which may be used in combination with the process modeling and management principles of human interaction management.

B. What are the Basic areas of IT Project Management?

Project Management is composed of several different types of activities such as:
Planning the work or objectives
Analysis & Design of objectives
Assessing and mitigating risk
Estimating resources
Allocation of resources
Organizing the work
Acquiring human and material resources
Assigning tasks
Directing activities
Controlling project execution
Tracking and Reporting progress
Analyzing the results based on the facts achieved
Defining the products of the project
Forecasting future trends in the project
Quality Management
Issues Management

C. Cross Cultural Factors in IT Project Management

Project Management South of the Border - A U.S. Project Manager's Perspective on Cultural Differences Affecting Projects in Mexico

Article Reference Material:

http://www.pmforum.org/library/papers/2006/08.htm#02

Question 1: Project Planning

How are projects planned?

A: The objective of a project is either to solve an existing problem or to start a new venture. In either case a carefully planned and organized strategy is needed to accomplish the specified objectives. The strategy includes developing a plan which will define the goals, explicitly set the tasks to be accomplished, determine how they will be accomplished, estimate time and the resources (both human and material) needed for their completion.

How projects are planned and managed will seriously impact on the profitability of the ventures that they are intended for and the quality of the products or services they generate.

Most project management plans are subdivided into four major phases: the feasibility study, the project planning, the project implementation and the verification or evaluation. Each one of these phases requires strategic planning.

Since all the tasks included in a project cannot be executed at the same time because of their interdependence, a critical path needs to be determined when scheduling of the activities.
The three major tools that are used for the purpose of planning and scheduling the different tasks in project management are the Gantt chart, the Critical Path Analysis (or Method) and the Program Evaluation and Review Technique.

But before any scheduling starts, it is essential to accurately estimate the time that every task might require. A good scheduling must take into account the possible unexpected events and the complexity involved in the tasks themselves.

This requires a thorough understanding of every aspect of the tasks before developing a list.
One way of creating a list of tasks is a process known as the Work Breakdown Structure (WBS). It consists in creating a tree of activities that take into account their lengths and contingence. The WBS starts with the project to be achieved and goes down to the different steps necessary for its completion. As the tree starts to grow, the list of the tasks grows.

Once the list of all the tasks involved is known, based on experience or good wit, an estimation of the time required can be made and milestones determined.

Knowing the milestones of a project with certainty is extremely important, because they can affect the timeliness of the project completion as a whole, and delays in project completions can have serious financial consequences and above all they can cost companies market shares. In a global competitive market, innovation is the driving force that keeps businesses alive, and this is more obvious in high tech industries. Most companies have several lines of products and each one of them is required to put out a new product every year or every six months. If for instance DELL's Inspiron or Latitude fails to put out new products on time, it is likely to lose profit from the forgone sales (the loss is proportional to the products' Time-To-Live) and market shares to its competitors.

The Gantt chart

Gantt charts (named after the American social scientist, Henry L. Gantt, its author) are effective for scheduling complex tasks. They help arrange the different events in synchronism and associate each task with its owner and its estimated beginning and ending time.

The charts also allow the project's team to visualize the resources need to complete the project and the timing for each task, it therefore shows where the task owners must be at any given time in the execution of the projects. The team working on the project should know whether it is on schedule or not by just looking at the chart.

The chart itself is divided in two parts. The first parts shows the different tasks, the tasks owners, the timing and the resources needed for their completion; the second part graphically visualizes the sequence of the events.

The following chart summarizes a project scheduling for a building construction.

The horizontal bars on the calendar side of the chart depict the beginnings and the ends of the scheduled tasks.

Some tasks cannot start until the preceding ones are finished. The main disadvantage of a Gantt chart is that it does not take into account the interdependence between the tasks. It shows the sequence and the beginning and the ends of the tasks but does not indicate whether one task has to wait for the end of a preceding one.

The Critical Path Analysis is another tool used for complex projects and it does take into account the interdependence of the tasks

Critical Path Analysis (CPA)

Not only does the CPA take into account the interdependence of the critical tasks, but in addition it considers the possibility of performing different tasks in parallel, and the tasks that can be performed at the same time or wait. It also helps monitor the execution of the tasks as they are being implemented. The CPA identifies the tasks that need to be completed on time and the ones that can wait for the whole project to meet its deadline. It helps estimate the Critical Path, the project duration and the slack time for every activity.

The CPA resembles the tree in the Work Breakdown Structure (WBS) with the difference that it takes into account the timing of the tasks. It is a web of activities linked by arrows between every two nodes.

The first step in creating a CPA diagram is to list the tasks including their duration and the order in which they have to be completed.

In some case, the project team might itself be in need to complete the project before the time predicted by the CPA, which creates a need to reduce the time spent on some activities.

The following table contains the information needed to create and display the Critical Path for a fictitious project.

Activity	Predecessor	Duration
A	NONE	3
B	A	5
C	A	3
D	B	5
E	C	6
F	D	7
G	E	4
H	G	2

Based on this information, we can determine the Critical Path, the project duration and the slack time for H.

Task A is the first on the list, no other task can start until it is completed. Tasks B and C come next, they are contingent on task A. Task E, G and H are on the same path as C, while task D and F are on the same path and depend on B.

The letters on the diagram represent the different activities and the numbers beside them represent the time it will take to accomplish the tasks.

The diagram shows that there are two paths to the project: ABDF and ACEGH. The duration for ABDF is 20 day and the duration for ACEGH is 18 days. Since ABDF is the longest path, it is also the Critical Path. The earliest that the task H can start is within 16 days.

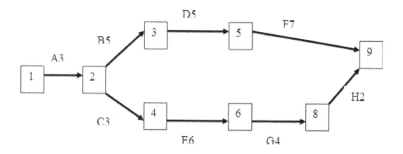

The advantage of the Gantt chart over the CPA is the graphical visualization of the tasks along with their timing, the task owners, the start time and end times. The advantage of the CPA over the Gantt chart is the sequence of events that takes into account the interdependence of the tasks.

The CPA is a deterministic model because it does not take into account the probability for the tasks to be completed sooner or later than expected, the time variation is not considered.

Program Evaluation and Review Technique (PERT)

The PERT is just a variation of the CPA with the difference that it follows a probabilistic approach while the CPA is a deterministic model.

Once the critical tasks have been identified, their timing estimated, the sequence of events determined and a list of activities established, we can evaluate the probability for

the different tasks to be accomplished on time and the shortest possible time for each of them.
The completion of each task is said to follow a Beta distribution with the expected length of the project being

$$E(p) = \frac{LgT + ST + 4 * lt}{6}$$

Where
LgT stands for Longest time
ST Stands for Shortest time
lt Stands for likely time

The estimated standard deviation $\sigma = \dfrac{LgT - ST}{6}$

The completion of the whole project follows a Normal distribution.
Based on the information bellow, find the critical path for the project, the project completion time, the probability of finishing it on time and the probability of finishing it at least 1 day earlier.

Activity	Predecessor	Most likely time	Shortest time	Longest time
A	NONE	3	2	4
B	A	5	4	6
C	A	3	2	4
D	B	5	3	6
E	C	6	5	6
F	D	7	5	8
G	E	4	3	4
H	G	2	1	3

Solution:

Activity	Predecessor	Most likely time	Shortest time	Longest time	Estimated mean	Standard Deviation	Variance
A	NONE	3	2	4	3	.17	.029
B	A	5	4	6	5	.33	.11
C	A	3	2	4	3	.33	.11
D	B	5	3	6	4.8	.5	.25
E	C	6	5	6	5.83	.17	.029
F	D	7	5	8	6.83	.33	.11
G	E	4	3	4	3.83	.17	.029
H	G	2	1	3	2	.33	.33

The critical path has the longest duration. It is critical because any delay in any task will cause a delay for the whole project. In this case, we have two paths ABDF which will last 20 days and ACEGH which will last 17 days. So the critical path is ABDF.

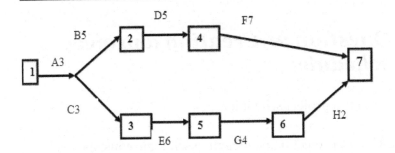

The estimated variance for the critical path is 0.029 + 0.11 + 0.25 + 0.11 = 0.499 with a standard deviation of $\sqrt{0.499} = 0.706$.

Completing the project at least 1 day earlier means completing it in 19 days or less. The probability for such an event to take place is found using Normal distribution

$$z = \frac{19 - 20}{0.706} = -1.416$$

1.42 corresponds to 0.9222 on the Normal table. Since we have a negative sign, the area we are looking for will be on the right side of 0.9222 under the normal curve which is equal to 0.0778.

Question 2: Creating a project schedule

What is a project schedule?

A1: In project management, a schedule consists of a list of a project's terminal elements with intended start and finish dates.

A Gantt chart can provide a graphical representation of a project schedule.

Critical chain project management warns that terminal-element start dates and finish dates function as random variables, and suggests managing a project not by its traditional schedule but rather by using buffer management and a relay race mentality.

Before a project schedule can be created, a project manager should typically have a work breakdown structure (WBS), an effort estimate for each task, and a resource list with availability for each resource. If these are not yet available, it may be possible to create something that looks like a schedule, but it will essentially be a work of fiction. They can be created using a consensus-driven estimation method like Wideband Delphi. The reason for this is that a schedule itself is an estimate: each date in the schedule is estimated, and if those dates do not have the buy-in of the people who are going to do the work, the schedule will be inaccurate.

Many project scheduling software products exist which can do much of the tedious work of calculating the schedule automatically, and plenty of books and tutorials dedicated to teaching people how to use them. However, before a project manager can use these tools, he or she should understand the concepts behind the WBS, dependencies, resource allocation, critical paths, Gantt charts and earned value. These are the real keys to planning a successful project.

A2: A project is said to consist of a collection of independent activities, or jobs. These activities can be represented in the form of a network. Such an approach has been commonly used to study project scheduling [1-4].

If one job needs to be completed before another can begin, we say the first job is an immediate predecessor of the job following, or equivalently, the latter in an immediate successor of the former. This predecessor relationship can be shown by a project graph or network. These graphs can basically be drawn in two ways:

1. Arrow Diagram: The arrow diagram shows the jobs as arrows connecting two nodes, and the immediate predecessor relationship is denoted by the predecessor's terminal node being identical with its successor's initial node. 'Dummy jobs' might need to be added sometimes to construct an arrow diagram if two or more activities in the project have identical immediate predecessors and successors, or if two or more jobs have some, but not all, of their immediate predecessors in common.

Figure 1: Two-activity Example - AOA Diagram

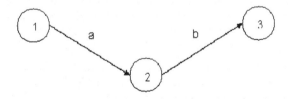

2. Activity-on-node graph: The jobs are portrayed by nodes and the immediate predecessor relation between two jobs by an arrow from the node representing the predecessor to the node representing the successor. Using this graph normally helps avoiding the addition of cumbersome dummy jobs to an arrow diagram.

Figure 2: Two-activity Example – AON Diagram

1.1.1 The notion of Critical Path

Once we have reduced a project to a network of activities and events and have estimated the activity durations, we are in a position to determine the minimum time required for the completion of the entire project. To do so, we must find the longest path, or the sequence of connected activities, through the network.

This is called the critical path of the network and its length determines the duration of the project. To illustrate this concept, we can take an example.

Suppose we have two salesmen who have a meeting in San Francisco one evening. They discover that they are both going to Los Angles the next day and agree to continue their conversation the next day. One of the salesmen Mr. Allen lives in Santa Barbara and plans to go through that city, have lunch with this wife, and then travel to Los Angeles. Mr. Baker, the other salesman, has an appointment with a client for lunch in Bakersfield and must go there on the way to Los Angeles. They would both like to meet as early as possible the next day.

The driving time from San Francisco to Los Angeles is about 8 hours if one goes through Bakersfield and about 11 hours if one goes through Santa Barbara. Moreover, we assume that both of them will spend 2 hours for lunch. Now we can describe their travel to Los Angeles as a project whose final event is their meeting for dinner.

The routes which the two gentlemen shall take can be given as:

Figure 3: Routes from San Francisco to Los Angeles

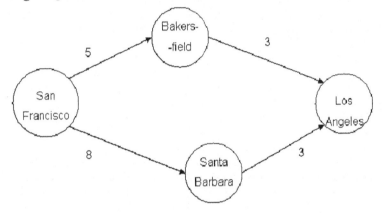

The project activities and immediate predecessors can be listed as follows.

Table 1: Project of traveling to Los Angeles

Job Name	Alternate	Job Description	Immediate Predecessors	Time (hours)
A	(1,2)	Allen drives from San Francisco to Santa Barbara	-	8
B	(2,3)	Allen lunches with wife	A	2
C	(3,6)	Allen drives from Santa Barbara to Los Angeles	B	3
D	(1,4)	Baker drives from San Francisco to Bakersfield	-	5
E	(4,5)	Baker lunches with customer	D	2
F	(5,6)	Baker drives from Bakersfield to Los Angeles	E	3

The arrow diagram for this project can finally be drawn as:

Figure 4: AOA Diagram for the project of traveling to Los Angeles

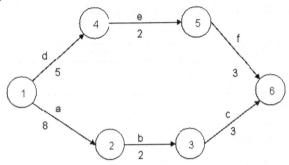

From the diagram, we can see that Allen will take 13 hours (along the route 1-2-3-6) while Baker will take 10 hours (along the route 1-4-5-6). Hence here Allen's path is critical. Baker can leave 3 hours later than Allen, or extend his lunch by 3 hours and still make it to Los Angeles for their meeting in time. Hence we can say that Baker has some slack in his path, or more generally speaking, jobs not on the critical path have slack.

Such information is extremely useful to project managers because it tells them how much flexibility they have in scheduling various jobs. Algorithms have been designed to estimate the critical paths once the activity diagrams and job durations are known.

The model encoded in the software LINGO for a project involving the roll-out of a new product. PERT is a particularly useful at identifying the critical activities within the project, which if delayed, will delay the project as a whole. The path comprising of these non-slack activities is the critical path for the network.

Now a certain company wants to launch a new product. In order to guarantee the launch occurring in time, PERT analysis is made of the tasks leading up to the launch. The tasks that must be accomplished before introduction and their anticipated times for completion are as follows:

Table 2: Tasks involved and time required

Task	Weeks
Finalize Design	10
Forecast Demand	14
Survey Competition	3
Set prices	3
Schedule Production Run	7
Cost Out	4
Train Salesmen	10

Now certain tasks must be completed before others can commence. These precedence relations can be shown by the following graph.

Figure 5: Product launch precedence relations

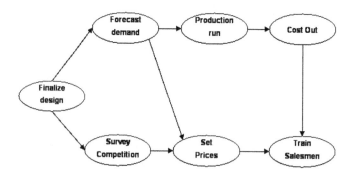

The following is the LINGO code [1] for determination of the critical path for the above network.

Figure 6: Coding for critical path evaluation sets: tasks / design, forecast, survey, price, schedule, costout, train/: time, ES, LS, slack;

```
pred(tasks, tasks) /
design,forecast,
design,survey,
forecast,price,
forecast,schedule,
survey,price,
schedule,costout,
price,train,
costout,train /;
endsets

data:
time = 10, 14, 3, 3, 7, 4, 10;
enddata

@for(tasks(j)|j #GT# 1:
ES(j) = @MAX(pred(i,j) : ES(i) + time(i))
);
@for(tasks(i)|i #LT# ltask:
LS(i) =  @min(pred(i,j) : LS(j) - time(i));
);
@for(tasks(i):slack(i) = LS(i)-ES(i));

ES (1) = 0;
ltask = @size(tasks);
LS(ltask) = ES(ltask);
```

The results as obtained for this model are:
Figure 7: Results obtained through LINGO
Feasible solution found.
Total solver iterations: 0

Variable	Value
LTASK	7.000000
TIME(DESIGN)	10.00000
TIME(FORECAST)	14.00000
TIME(SURVEY)	3.000000
TIME(PRICE)	3.000000
TIME(SCHEDULE)	7.000000
TIME(COSTOUT)	4.000000
TIME(TRAIN)	10.00000
ES(DESIGN)	0.000000
ES(FORECAST)	10.00000
ES(SURVEY)	10.00000
ES(PRICE)	24.00000
ES(SCHEDULE)	24.00000
ES(COSTOUT)	31.00000
ES(TRAIN)	35.00000
LS(DESIGN)	0.000000
LS(FORECAST)	10.00000
LS(SURVEY)	29.00000
LS(PRICE)	32.00000
LS(SCHEDULE)	24.00000
LS(COSTOUT)	31.00000
LS(TRAIN)	35.00000
SLACK(DESIGN)	0.000000
SLACK(FORECAST)	0.000000
SLACK(SURVEY)	19.00000
SLACK(PRICE)	8.000000
SLACK(SCHEDULE)	0.000000
SLACK(COSTOUT)	0.000000
SLACK(TRAIN)	0.000000

The continuous activities with slack as zero would
comprise the critical path.

1.1.2 PERT and CPM

Both CPM and PERT use the project network [2]. It is the basis of both techniques, and the notions of critical path and activity slack are common to each. They differ however in the fact that they were developed independently and in somewhat different problem settings. In actual application though, some of their differences have disappeared or at least become less significant.

PERT was developed for and has been used most frequently in the aerospace industry, notably in the research and development type of programs. These industries are relatively new, their technologies rapidly changing, and their products non-standard.

CPM, on the other hand, has most frequently been applied to construction projects. They employ long-developed and well-seasoned components, and they are based on a more or less stable technology.

Another difference between PERT and CPM could be that CPM is 'activity-oriented' while PERT is often 'event-oriented'. An activity represents a segment of work to be finished over a period of time, but an event is a point in time, a milestone representing the beginning or the completion of some activity or group of activities. The emphasis on events thus has its roots in the milestone method of management, in which the program progress is measured in terms of success or failure in reaching certain important milestones at the scheduled points in time.

PERT
Hence there is a large amount of uncertainty in the PERT projects – uncertainty about the time required for developmental research, engineering design, and ultimate construction; about the specific activities and sometimes about the configuration of the end product itself. Hence PERT takes some of these uncertainties into account.

It essentially utilizes a probabilistic model making an estimate of the most probable time required to complete an activity and also the measure of uncertainty possible in this estimate. A pessimistic estimate, which is the best guess of the maximum time that would be required to complete the activity if bad luck was encountered at every stage of its completion, and an optimistic estimate, which is the minimum time that the activity would take if everything goes fine, are made. After this, the expected, or average, time estimate is made using probability distribution.

CPM

CPM was originally developed to solve scheduling problems in an industrial setting. For this reason, it is less concerned with uncertainty problems that PERT attempts to cope with and focuses instead on the costs of project scheduling and how to minimize them.

Thus unlike PERT which used a probabilistic model, CPM utilizes a "deterministic model" instead. It does allow for variations in job times, not as a result of random factors though, but as the planned and expected outcome of resource assignments.

Most jobs, CPM argues, can be reduced in duration if extra resources are assigned to them. The cost for getting the job done may increase, but the other advantages outweigh this added cost, and the job is expedited or crashed. If a job has a generous amount of slack though, it can be performed at a slower or more efficient pace. Thus it provides the trade off between the costs and project durations.

1.2 Project scheduling with constrained resources

During the development of PERT and CPM networks, we have generally assumed that sufficient resources are available to perform various activities. At a certain time, the demand for a particular resource is the cumulative demand for that resource on all the activities being performed at that time.

The demand for a certain type of resource may fluctuate from very high at one time to very low at another. If it is a material or unskilled labor, which has to be procured from time to time, the fluctuation in demand will not significantly affect the cost of the project. However, if it is some personnel who cannot be hired and fired during the project or machines, which are to be hired for the total project duration, the fluctuation in their demand will affect the total project cost due to high idle times.

To reduce the idle period, the activities on non-critical paths are shifted by making use of certain techniques and alternate schedule is generated comparing the important resources, with the object of smoothening the demand for resources. In some situations, we may be faced with a demand for some critical resource, which may be limited in supply. For example, the only technician available may be needed for two activities at two places at the same time. This makes the schedule infeasible and calls for a re-examination with the object of generating an alternate plan with feasible scheduling of the limited resource.

Thus, the object of resource scheduling is two-fold:
- Bringing down the costs and at the same time
- Reduction of pressure on the limited resources in conflicting demands

The resource-scheduling situation depends upon the type of constraint:

Total project duration: In this case, the resource scheduling only smoothens the demand for resources in order that the demand for any resource is as uniform as possible. This type of resource scheduling is called resource smoothening or load smoothening.

Availability of certain resources: Here the project duration is not treated as an invariant, but the demand for certain specified resources should not go beyond the specified level. This operation of resource allocation is called resource leveling or load leveling.

A step of methodologies is employed to solve this kind of a problem. The main steps are:

Resource Aggregation: Beginning from the network diagram assuming unlimited resources, an estimate of the number of men required for performing the activities scheduled for each day are made. This is the requirement of resources for the project to be completed in the minimum possible time.

The availability of the resource could however be less than the requirement during certain periods of time for which resource leveling shall have to be done extending the length of the project.

Resource Leveling: These programs attempt to reduce peak resource requirements and smooth out the period-to-period assignments, within a constraint on project duration.

Resource Allocation: These programs allocate available resources to project activities in an attempt to find the shortest project schedule consistent with fixed resource limits.

The Complexity of Project Scheduling with Limited Resources

Activities requiring the same set of limited resources in such models have to be scheduled so that no two of them requiring the same facility occur at the same time. Or if there are a relatively small number of resources, their limited availability must be jointly considered while scheduling.

At the other extreme are projects requiring many resources, most of which are available in fixed and limited amounts. The problem of scheduling activities such that none of the resource availabilities are exceeded and none of the precedence relationships are violated is an exceedingly difficult task for projects even of a modest size. This is especially true if one tries to minimize project duration or meet some other reasonable scheduling criteria.

Scheduling projects with limited resources is mathematically a large combinatorial problem. There are a very large number of combinations of activity start times, each combination representing a different schedule, too large to compute even with a very big computer. Analytical computations are hence computationally impractical for most real-life problems.

Question 3: Work Breakdown Structure (WBS)

How are WBS created?

A: In project management, a Work Breakdown Structure (WBS) is an exhaustive, hierarchical (from general to specific) tree structure of deliverables and tasks that need to be performed to complete a project. The Work Breakdown Structure is a very common and critical project management tool. It is considered such a key part of project management that many United States government statements of work require a WBS.

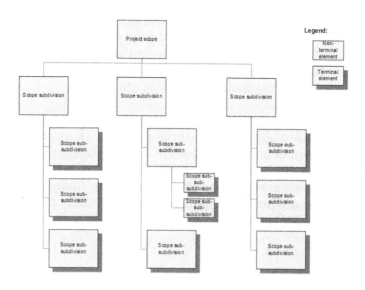

Example of a simple work breakdown structure.

The purpose of a WBS is to document the scope of a project. Its hierarchical arrangement allows for easy identification of the terminal elements (the actual items to be done in a project). Being an exhaustive document of the project scope, the WBS serves as the basis (indeed, the backbone) for much of project planning. All the work to be done in a project must trace its origin from one or more WBS entries.

How to build a WBS

A WBS is simply an organized presentation of the work required to complete the project. There are any number of ways to organize the presentation of the work. For example, one could organize it according to life-cycle phases, showing each phase as a top-level breakdown. Another way to organize it is by functional responsibilities. A key thing to remember is that the WBS documents the scope of the project, and not the execution plan of the project. Thus, in the house painting example below, 'Prepare Materials' could appear after 'Paint the Room' and it is still a valid and correct WBS.

(For more details on the various approaches to building the WBS for a project see e.g. How to Build a Work Breakdown Structure below.)

Whether the WBS should be activity-oriented or deliverable-oriented is a subject of much discussion. Even suggesting picking one style and then sticking to it can be a point of argument.

An example of a work breakdown for painting a room (activity-oriented) is, to state the obvious:
Prepare materials
Buy paint
Buy a ladder
Buy brushes/rollers
Buy wallpaper remover
Prepare room

Remove old wallpaper
Remove detachable decorations
Cover floor with old newspapers
Cover electrical outlets/switches with tape
Cover furniture with sheets
Paint the room
Clean up the room
Dispose or store left over paint
Clean brushes/rollers
Dispose of old newspapers
Remove covers

For comparative purposes, a deliverable-oriented WBS might look something like:
Material Preparation
Paint preparation
Ladder preparation
Brushes/rollers preparation
Wallpaper Remover
Room Preparation
Old wallpaper removal
Detachable decorations removal
Floor protection
Electrical outlets/switches protection
Furniture protection
Room Painting
Room cleanup
Leftover paint disposal
Brushes/rollers cleaning
Old newspapers disposal
Covers removal

Level of detail

There is no set depth or breadth specifications for a WBS. The context determines if your WBS is too general, or too detailed. Project management is not about performing the work, but rather more concerned about monitoring the work, so a good maxim to follow in preparing the WBS is to go to just enough detail to allow a piece of work to assigned to a resource, and then the status monitored. Of course, there is nothing to stop that resource from developing their own WBS for the work assigned to them.

The size of the WBS should generally not exceed 100-200 terminal elements (if more terminal elements seem to be required, use subprojects). The WBS should be up to 3-4 levels deep. Each level should be 5-9 elements broad. These suggestions derive from the following facts:

short-term memory capacity is limited to 5-9 items. Having fixed time to plan a project, the more terminal elements there are, the less time there is to pay attention to any single one of them. Consequently, the estimates are less thought-through.
The more terminal elements there are the more there are potential dependencies among them (see fact 2 above for consequences).

It is common practice, in medium-sized to large projects, to use a hierarchical coding system, assigning a code to each WBS entry. A top level entry might have (for example) a code of 1, 2, 3, and so on, while entries under entry 1 may have codes from 1.1, 1.2, 1.3, etc.

Tools for developing a WBS

Project management software, can be very helpful in developing a WBS, although in early stages of WBS development, plain sticky notes are hard to beat for flexibility. It is much easier for a team to work together using sticky notes and a large empty wall than for the same team to cram themselves in front of a tiny computer monitor and one keyboard.

Example of a detailed work breakdown structure

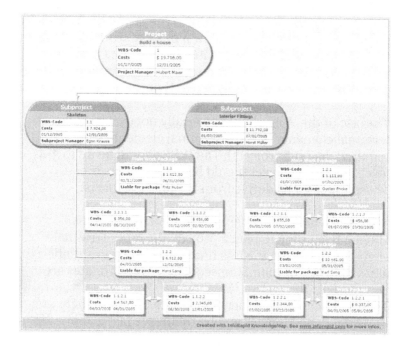

Question 4: Basic Project Documents

What are the Basic Project Documents needed to start a project?

A: During project start, some documents have to be secured first. The basic documents needed are as follows:

Project Design and Concept
Approved Project Proposal consisting of General and Specific Objective

After the two basic documents have been finalized, other project documents should follow soon. These are as follows:

1. Project Charter
2. Business case/Feasibility Study
3. Scope Statement
4. Work Breakdown Structure
5. Change Control Plan
6. Risk Management Plan
7. Communications Plan
6. Governance Model
7. Risk Register
8. Issue Log
9. Resource Management Plan
10. Project Schedule
11. Status Report
12. Gantt Chart
13. Responsibility assignment matrix
14. Database of risks
15. Database of lessons learned
16. Stakeholder Analysis

Some of the documents cited above may be produced during project implementation and can be edited or appended during the implementation phases of the project. It all depends on a lot of factors and considerations during project monitoring and results of period assessments and planning.

Question 5: Project Accounting

What is Project Accounting?

A: Project accounting is the practice of creating financial reports specifically designed to track the financial progress of projects, which can then be used by managers to aid project management.

Standard accounting is primarily aimed at monitoring financial progress of organizational elements (geographical or functional departments, divisions and the enterprise as a whole) over defined time periods (typically weeks, months, quarters and years).

Projects differ in that they frequently cross organizational boundaries, may last for anything from a few days or weeks to a number of years, during which time budgets may also be revised many times. They may also be one of a number of projects that make up a larger overall project or program.

Consequently, in a project management environment costs and revenues are also allocated to projects, which may be subdivided into a work breakdown structure, and grouped together into project hierarchies. Project accounting permits reporting at any such level that has been defined, and often allows comparison with historical as well as current budgets.

Where labor costs are a significant portion of overall project cost, it is usually necessary for employees to fill out a timesheet in order to generate the data to allocate project costs.

The capital budget processes of corporations and governments are chiefly concerned with major investment projects that typically have upfront costs and longer term benefits. Investment go / no-go decisions are largely based on net present value assessments. Project accounting of the costs and benefits can provide crucially important feedback on the quality of these important decisions.

An interesting specialized form of project accounting is production accounting, which tracks the costs of individual movie and television episode film production costs. A movie studio will employ production accounting to track the costs of its many separate projects.

Question 6: Capability Maturity Model (CMM)

What is CMM?

A: The Capability Maturity Model describes a continuum of five stages based on how well a company or organization follows common and repeatable processes to get work done. The low end of the scale describes companies without repeatable processes, where much of the work is chaotic and ad-hoc. The highest end describes companies that use defined and repeatable processes, collect metrics to help them continuously improve their processes, and look for creative ways to do things better on an ongoing basis.

The CMM was developed from 1984 to 1987 by Watts Humphrey and the Software Engineering Institute (SEI). The SEI is a part of Carnegie Mellon University. The work was funded, and continues to be funded, by the Department of Defense (DoD), which was originally looking for ways to compare and measure the various contractors that were developing software for the DoD. Although the SEI continues to enhance and expand the scope and breadth of various CMM models, the primary focus for most companies continues to be the software development world.

The Capability Maturity Model contains five stages to evaluate how sophisticated your organization is in establishing and following standard processes.

The Five-Stage Capability Maturity Model (CMM) (0.0.1.1.P2)

There are some slightly different interpretations of the CMM. Some companies have also identified their own proprietary versions of the CMM process. However, in general, there are five defined stages.

Ad-hoc/crises. Your organization has few common processes. The success of your projects depends on the strength and skills of your people. The organization provides little in a supporting environment to help make all projects successful. Most companies are at this level; although some companies say half-jokingly that they are at a 0 or even a -1 level.

Standard project management. Your organization has implemented standard project management processes, and you utilize these common processes on all projects. You are trying to establish a baseline foundation upon which to improve further in the future. Most companies that start down the CMM path are trying to reach this level.

Standard software development. You are trying to achieve standardization in your development process similar to what you did for project management in level 2. This includes common and repeatable software development processes, deliverables, tools, etc.

Managed feedback. You collect metrics on all aspects of your project management and development processes. You have a repository of metrics and key learnings on historical projects that can be leveraged by new projects.

Optimizing / continuous improvement. You have a closed loop of process execution, measurement and continuous improvement. You continuously use measurement, feedback and creativity to optimize your processes.
Is CMM Right for You?

Should your company start down the CMM road? Just as there are real benefits to reusing common software components, there is also value in reusing common processes. Why should every project manager in your company struggle to understand how to define a project and how detailed the workplan should be? Why should project managers struggle to understand how to effectively manage scope, risks and quality? These are not new concepts, even within your own company. These processes should all be defined once at an organizational level and then reused by all project managers.

You can use the CMM model as your guide as you try to implement common processes. You don't have to start from level 1 and jump to level 5 in one year. The CMM scale is a journey. Most companies only want to start by moving to level 2. However, even that short jump is not without pain. In many respects, implementing common project management processes is the most difficult part of the journey. In many organizations, this is the first time people will be asked to follow a common set of processes and many won't like it. If you can successfully get to level 2, then you should have already established the paradigm shift that will make the transition to level 3 a little easier.

In general then, many companies are seeing that they can drive business value by implementing good, reusable processes throughout their organization. The Capability Maturity Model provides a framework that companies can use to measure themselves on a standard 1 - 5 scale. Most companies today are at level 1 and would love to get as high as level 2. Most managers and most organizations realize that they should have common and repeatable processes However, there is definitely pain involved. There is pain involved with all culture change initiatives when you ask people to change how they do their jobs. However, the pain can definitely be worth the gain, if your company can stay focused for the time it will take for the culture change to take effect.

Question 7: The Value of Project Lifecycle Methodology

What is the value of Project Lifecycle Methodology?

A: There are some companies that have built reputations for being able to consistently manage projects effectively. However, the vast majority of organizations have a more spotty reputation. A lot of the blame for these problems can be traced back to a lack of project management processes and discipline. However, typically if a company lacks processes for project management, they also are not going to have a standard process for the project lifecycle either. In fact, much of the value of project management comes from its application across the lifecycle. The following examples should help illustrate this:

The initial parts of project management focus on defining the work and building a workplan. The workplan is going to be focused on executing the project using a lifecycle model. Even if you have great project management processes in place, you still need to know the basic models for the lifecycle. If you are not clear how you will execute the project, you are going to have faulty estimates and a poor workplan.

After the project is defined you need to manage it using project management process. Many of these processes are based on the lifecycle. For instance, problems are going to arise during the execution of the project that will require issues management. There are going to be quality control and quality assurance processes in place. Some of these will focus on the project management processes, but most of the quality control work, and much of the quality assurance work, will be focused on lifecycle activities. Likewise, most of the aspects of risk will be related to project execution and project deliverables. Risk

47

management is a project management function, but its application on a project will typically be in relation to executing the lifecycle.

Managing people is a project management function. However, except for the project manager, the project team members are all going to be executing various parts of the lifecycle. So the application of people management during the project will be in relation to the lifecycle. If you do not understand the lifecycle required for your project, you are going to have problems managing the project team, assigning them the right work and dealing with their concerns.

Project teams cannot be totally successful unless they understand the project lifecycle that is applicable to their project. There are many ways to execute a project most of which provide for a less than optimum solution. Using standard lifecycle processes and techniques help you coordinate resources to achieve predictable results. However, it should be understood up front that the lifecycle is not totally a science, and there is never a guarantee of success. Since projects involve people, there is always complexity and uncertainty that cannot be absolutely controlled. Building and managing according to a lifecycle model is partly an art that requires flexibility and creativity. A good lifecycle process provides the framework, processes, guidelines and techniques to structure the work. A good lifecycle increases the odds of being successful, and therefore provides value to the organization, project and the project team.

The value proposition for utilizing a standard lifecycle process goes something like this. It takes time and effort to understand and utilize a standard project lifecycle across the entire organization. This cost is more than made up for over the life of the project by:

- Ensuring that all of the necessary work is included in the initial estimates and the initial workplan.

- Allowing the use of a standard lifecycle model that may account for the majority of the work required for your project. This increases the start-up time required for your project.

- Helping ensure that planning is done before execution in all steps of the lifecycle. This cuts down on misdirected work and rework.

Using standard templates and processes gets everyone in the organization comfortable with the major deliverables required on a project and the general flow of the project, again resulting in a faster startup time.

People who complain that lifecycle methodology is a lot of 'overhead' forget the point. Your project needs to utilize some type of lifecycle process. The question is whether you will learn from and take advantage of pre-existing processes and templates, or whether you will attempt to invent everything from scratch. Although every project is unique, the lifecycle model typically is not. The general lifecycle model you use will probably be similar to one that has been used dozens (or hundreds) or time at your company before, and millions of times in other organizations. There is no reason to reinvent everything for your project. It just takes longer and contains more inherent risk. The better approach is to utilize a standard set of lifecycle processes, techniques and templates.

After reading this section so far, you might wonder why everyone does not utilize a standard lifecycle process. Or you might think about yourself. Why aren't you using them? There are probably a couple reasons.

Good lifecycle processes require an upfront investment of time and effort for analysis and planning.
Many people consider themselves to be 'doers'. They might not be as comfortable with their analysis, design and planning skills. Many times there is a tendency to be handed a problem, and then go out and fix it. This works when you have a five-hour change request. It doesn't work on a 5,000 hour project. Resist the urge to jump right in. The project will complete sooner if you properly plan it first, understand the requirements correctly and design an efficient solution. This should result is vastly reducing the time, effort and rework required in the Construct, Test and Implement Phases.

Your organization is not committed.
It's hard to utilize good lifecycle skills in an organization that doesn't value the skills. For instance, if you take the time to formally document the business requirements, and your client asks why you were wasting your time doing it, then you probably are not going to be very excited about formally documenting the requirements on your next project. To be effective, the entire organization must support a common set of processes and models.

You don't know how to.
You may find that the lack of lifecycle processes is not a matter of will, but a matter of skill. Sometimes people are asked to manage and execute projects without the training or the experience necessary. In those cases, they struggle without the right tools or training to execute their projects effectively.

Senior managers think that lifecycle management is a tool.
When you discuss the project lifecycle with some managers,

they initially think you are trying to implement a tool. Actually there are many aspects of the lifecycle that can be supported by tools. These range from gathering business requirements and creating models down to the testing and implementation process. However, tools are only part of the answer. Tools are best used to automate features of the lifecycle that are very large or very tedious. It makes sense, for instance, to automate the modeling process since tools are much easier to utilize than building models by hand. Likewise, testing typically requires the tedious application of a vast amount of data. The testing process is a good candidate for tools as well. However, tools support your project lifecycle methodology. They are not a substitute.

You may have been burned (or buried) in the past. A common criticism of methodology is that it is cumbersome, paper intensive and takes too much focus away from the work at hand. Sometimes this criticism is a feature of the first bullet point above. Other times, it is a legitimate concern, caused by not scaling the methodology to the size of your project. For instance, if you were required to develop Testing and Training Strategy documents for projects that were only 100 effort hours, you may have been turned off. However, this is not usually a methodology problem as much as it is a misapplication of the methodology.

Some of these fears are natural and logical, while others are emotional and irrational. Although these may be reasons to be hesitant about using formal lifecycle project lifecycle process, they must be overcome. When you use a lifecycle process, be smart. Don't build the project workplan for a ten million dollar project if your project is only ten thousand dollars. Consider all the aspects of your project, and build the right processes for your specific project.

Options for Obtaining a Methodology

To successfully implement a lifecycle methodology, first convince yourself that there is value if the process is applied and utilized correctly. In fact, all projects use a methodology of processes, procedures and templates. If you don't think you have one, it really means that you have a poor and informal one.

If you need a good lifecycle methodology, there are two major sources.

Build one yourself. You can build a custom methodology that perfectly reflects the philosophy and best practices of your organization. Many companies continue to do this today.

Buy one. If you build a methodology, you might be surprised to learn that it ultimately looks similar to most other lifecycle methodologies that people use. No matter how you structure it, you still need to do some level of analysis, design, construct, test and implement. Therefore, many companies chose an option to buy or license a pre-existing methodology. These pre-built methodologies usually have everything your organization needs to be successful.

There is also the hybrid option of purchasing a methodology and then customizing it to meet the specific needs of your organization. This gives you some of the benefits of option 1, while also taking less time, which is the major benefit of option 2.

Question 8: Project Roles and Responsibilities

What are the different project roles and responsibilities?

A: Projects of different sizes have different ways and requirements on how the people are organized. In a small project, little organization structure is needed. There might be a primary sponsor, project manager and a project team. However, for large projects, there are more and more people involved, and it is important that people understand what they are expected to do, and what role people are expected to fill. This section identifies some of the common (and not so common) project roles that may need to be required for your project.

Analyst. The analyst is responsible for ensuring that the requirements of the business clients are captured and documented correctly before a solution is developed and implemented. In some companies, this person might be called a Business Analyst, Business Systems Analyst, Systems Analyst or a Requirements Analyst. For more information on this role see 407.2 The Role of an Analyst.

Change Control Board. The Change Control Board is usually made up as a group of decision makers authorized to accept changes to the projects requirements, budget, and timelines. This organization would be helpful if the project directly impacted a number of functional areas and the sponsor wanted to share the scope change authority with this broader group. The details of the Change Control Board and the processes they follow are defined in the project management processes.

Client. This is the people (or groups) that are the direct beneficiaries of a project or service. They are the people for whom the project is being undertaken. (Indirect beneficiaries are probably stakeholders.) These might also be called "customers", but if they are internal to the company LifecycleStep refers to them generically as clients. If they are outside your company, they would be referred to as "customers".

Client Project Manager. If the project is large enough, the client may have a primary contact that is designated as a comparable project manager. As an example, if this were an IT project, the IT project manager would have overall responsibility for the IT solution. However, there may also be projects on the client side that are also needed to support the initiative, and the client project manager would be responsible for those. The IT project manager and the client project manager would be peers who work together to build and implement the complete solution.

Designer. The Designer is responsible for understanding the business requirements and designing a solution that will meet the business needs. There are many potential solutions that will meet the client's needs. The designer determines the best approach. A designer typically needs to understand how technology can be used to create this optimum solution for the client. The designer determines the overall model and framework for the solution, down to the level of designing screens, reports, programs and other components. They also determine the data needs. The work of the designer is then handed off to the programmers and other people who will construct the solution based on the design specifications.

Project Manager. This is the person with authority to manage a project. This includes leading the planning and the development of all project deliverables. The project manager is responsible for managing the budget and workplan and all project management procedures (scope management, issues management, risk management, etc.).

Project Team. The project team consists of the full-time and part-time resources assigned to work on the deliverables of the project. This includes the analysts, designers, programmers, etc. They are responsible for:

- Understanding the work to be completed
- Planning out the assigned activities in more detail if needed
- Completing assigned work within the budget, timeline and quality expectations
- Informing the project manager of issues, scope changes, risk and quality concerns
- Proactively communicating status and managing expectations

The project team can consist of human resources within one functional organization, or it can consist of members from many different functional organizations. A cross-functional team has members from multiple organizations. Having a cross-functional team is usually a sign of your organization utilizing matrix management.

Sponsor (Executive Sponsor and Project Sponsor). This is the person who has ultimate authority over the project. The Executive Sponsor provides project funding, resolves issues and scope changes, approves major deliverables and provides high-level direction. They also champion the project within their organization. Depending on the project, and the organizational level of the Executive Sponsor, they may delegate day-to-day tactical management to a Project Sponsor. If assigned, the Project Sponsor represents the Executive Sponsor on a day-to-day basis, and makes most of the decisions requiring sponsor approval. If the decision is large enough, the Project Sponsor will take it to the Executive Sponsor for resolution.

Stakeholder. These are the specific people or groups who have a stake, or an interest, in the outcome of the project. Normally stakeholders are from within the company, and could include internal clients, management, employees, administrators, etc. A project may also have external stakeholders, including suppliers, investors, community groups and government organization.

Steering Committee. A Steering Committee is a group of high-level stakeholders who are responsible for providing guidance on overall strategic direction. They do not take the place of a Sponsor, but help to spread the strategic input and buy-in to a larger portion of the organization. The Steering Committee is usually made up of organizational peers, and is a combination of direct clients and indirect stakeholders. The members on the Steering Committee may also sit on the Change Control Board, although in many cases the Change Board is made up of representatives of the Steering Committee.

Suppliers/Vendors. Although some companies may have internal suppliers, in the LifecycleStep Process, these terms will always refer to third party companies, or specific people that work for third parties. They may be subcontractors who are working under your direction, or they may be supplying material, equipment, hardware, software or supplies to your project. Depending on their role, they may need to be identified on your organization chart. For instance, if you are partnering with a supplier to develop your requirements, you probably want them on your organization chart. On the other hand, if they are a vendor supplying a common piece of hardware, you probably would not consider them a part of the team.

Users. These are the people who will actually use the deliverables of the project. These people are also involved heavily in the project in activities such as defining business requirements. In other cases, they may not get involved until the testing process. Sometimes you want to specifically identify the user organization or the specific users of the solution and assign a formal set of responsibilities to them, like developing use cases or user scenarios based on the needs of the business requirements.

Responsibility Matrix
In a large project, there may be many people who have some role in the creation and approval of project deliverables. Sometimes this is pretty straightforward, such as one person writing a document and one person approving it. In other cases, there may be many people who have a hand in the creation, and others that need to have varying levels of approval. The Responsibility Matrix is a technique used to define the general responsibilities for each role on a project. The matrix can then be used to communicate the roles to the appropriate people associated with the team. This helps set expectations, and ensures people know what is expected from them.

On the matrix, the different people, or roles, appear as columns, with the specific deliverables in question listed as rows. Then, use the intersecting points to describe each person's responsibility for each deliverable. A simple example matrix follows:

	Project Sponsor	Project Manager	Project Team	Client Managers	Analysts
Requirements Management Plan	A	C	R	A	R
Requirements Report	I, A	R	R	I, A	C
Process Model	R	R	R	I, A	C
Data Model	R	R	R	I, A	C
Requirements Traceability Matrix	R	R	R	R	C

A - Approves the deliverable
R - Reviews the deliverable (and provides feedback).
C - Creates the deliverable (could be C (1) for primary, C (2) for backup). Usually there is only one person who is responsible for creating a deliverable, although many people may provide input.
I - Provides input
N – Is notified when a deliverable is complete
M - Manages the deliverables (such as a librarian, or person responsible for the document repository)

In the table above, the Requirements Management Plan is created by the project manager, approved by the sponsor and client managers, and reviewed by the project team and analysts.

The purpose of the matrix is to gain clarity and agreement on who does what, so you can define the columns with as much detail as makes sense. For instance, in the above example, the 'Project Team' could have been broken into specific people or the person responsible for creating the Data Model could have been broken out into a separate column. After the matrix is completed, it should be circulated for approval. If it is done in the project definition process, it can be an addendum to the Project Definition. If it is created as a part of the initial Analysis Phase, it should be circulated as a separate document.

Examples of responsibility codes are as follows. Your project may define different codes, as long as you explain what they mean so that people know what the expectations are for them.

Question 9: Guidelines for formulating Mission, Vision, etc.

Are there any recommended websites, articles, authors, or organizations that you reference when working on the development of project, program, or corporate missions, visions, strategic statements, etc.?

A: Projects don't have to restrict themselves to advancing the corporate mission as John Herman somewhat implies:

"If a project does not address one of these points, is it worth doing at all?";

Some projects are performed simply to let the corporation meet regulatory or legal requirements.

I am reminded of the story of Nike. New hires were always invited to lunch with the president. He'd go round the table asking each person what his/her job was. At the end he'd tell them they were all wrong. "Your job can be summed up in two words: destroy Adidas."

I'll bet that wasn't in the corporate mission or value statement but it sure was the corporate ethos!

Seriously though, if your organization is only reputed to be a financial institution, what is it actually?

All of these mission and vision statements are just management make-work, something for a bunch of suits to congratulate themselves on as they sit in the board room wasting oxygen.

Any business can be divided into precisely two parts, money-makers and support. In your most classic business model, money-makers are sales and production. Without the sales people, you can't sell your product. Without production, you don't have a product to sell. This is what brings home the bacon. Any other department either helps or hinders this process.

IT, specifically SAP can provide the software to make sales and production more productive, thus increasing revenues. SAP can just as easily provide non-functional pieces of crap that leave those departments worse off than if they were still using paper.

Accounting and Finance can make sure the company's resources are efficiently allocated and utilized but they can just as easily demand so much documentation and pointless paperwork that the company would actually be saving money if they junked both departments and just put a bag of cash in the lunch room with a sign saying "take what you need."

Management is the biggest sinner of all. Management should be about serving the money-makers to keep the business healthy but they are under the mistaken impression that they themselves are the money-makers and it's the rest of the company holding them back. This sort of pig-headed, egocentric thinking is endemic in American industry. These are the same _ _ _ holes who think that they can outsource all production and still have a viable company. These are the same _ _ _ holes who think their 40 hour week is worth a compensation 500x greater than the 40 hour week of the line worker.

As for your mission statement, this one works for all circumstances: "Know who signs the check, know what they want you do to, do it well, and always look for ways to improve the process." Fill in the blanks for your particular business.

As for the sample outline, well here goes:

As a programmer, I would happily exchange every Project Plan with all their revisions for a good specification requirement document and a firm change management program.

1.0 GENERAL INFORMATION
   1.1 Purpose, Scope, and Objectives
   1.2 System Overview
   1.3 Contacts
   1.4 Project References
   1.5 Relationship to Other Projects
   1.6 Organizational Interfaces
   1.7 Acronyms and Abbreviations
2.0 PLANNED ACTIVITIES, EVENTS, AND DELIVERABLES
   2.1 Initiate Project Phase
   2.2 Define System Phase
   2.3 Design System Phase
   2.4 Build System Phase
   2.5 Evaluate System Phase
   2.6 Operate System Phase
3.0 RESOURCES
   3.1 Roles and Responsibilities
   3.2 Labor Categories
   3.3 Budget Estimates and Total Costs
      3.3.1 Estimates and Costs for Labor Categories
      3.3.2 Estimates and Costs for Capital Investments
      3.3.3 Estimates and Costs for Equipment
      3.3.4 Estimates and Costs for Operating Costs
      3.3.5 Estimates and Costs for Other Services
4.0 TECHNICAL APPROACH
   4.1 Methods and Techniques
   4.2 Environment
APPENDIX A: PROJECT SCHEDULE
APPENDIX B: LESSONS (not) LEARNED FROM EVERY OTHER PROJECT WE'VE EVER DONE

That said, the EPRI (Electric Power Research Institute)

Software Lifecycle Document Template would be my preferred poison, IF, like any other plan, it were followed and enforced.

Question 10: Business requirements and Project templates

I am starting a new project with a new company.

I need some information on best practices and styles to create/collect business requirements, designing business rules, branding etc.

Any samples or templates would be really helpful as a start.

Is there any guidance or service provider websites who can help you do project documentation?

A: The best thing I ever found is the UML and Use Case Modeling.

I would say some UML (Unified Modeling Language) and Use Cases would be good to have in Business Requirements, but you would need more then that. UML is definitely something you should have before you start coding though.

You first really just need to document what the client says they want into a readable format. After that you want to ask questions like how many users will this be for, who will use the application, how often will users use the program, will it be replacing an existing application, when do they want the project done, what roles/permissions will be required, and so on.

Question 11: Project Team

Assuming that you are to start a project with a free hand in selecting your team members, how would you go about it?

A: In organizations that are familiar with project management the selection of the team may have been completed at the same time as the project definition is produced. This may be because there is no choice about which resources will be used, because there are few of them to choose from, or because projects do not enter the definition phase unless the tacit approval of senior management has been given.

When this is not the case you may have to negotiate for resources with individual line managers and may even have to use the authority of senior managers to acquire your team. Avoid compromise when selecting resources; always strive to obtain the best people. You may not always be successful and you will be constantly surprised by the ability of those who were formerly considered 'second rankers'. So much so, that you may well reconsider your selection criteria for future projects.

When selecting the team you should consider skills, aptitude and personalities. If the team is to work well together there must be no strong clash of personalities. Occasionally, this will be unavoidable (see the Team Building Section of this document for tips about resolving conflict within the team).

Remember that suppliers and sub-contractors may also form part of the team. Make strenuous efforts to include the managers and staff of these organizations in the selection and teambuilding process. It will be poor consolation to have successfully negotiated your organizations 'A' team if the suppliers have fielded the 'C' team.

Team Building

1. Team Management

A project is delivered successfully by the project team. The project manager may be charismatic and enthusiastic but if the project team are immune to charisma and loathe enthusiasm then the project will suffer. It is the project manager's duty to deliver the project through the team and, therefore, the project manager must build the team so that they feel a responsibility to each and not just to the organization in order that they deliver the project to the defined requirements.

A project manager must be proficient at managing people but must never be seen as manipulative or deceitful. If the project manager does not have the authority of a line manager (which is often the case) or the responsibility for the team members' personal development then managing the team can be problematic, especially where there is no existing project management culture. This is most often the case when team members are only working part-time on the project. The authority of their operational line manager and the safe and familiar work will tempt some team members to give undue preference to operational work rather than the work of the project. Such situations are best dealt with through discussion with the line manager. The line manager's authority directing the team member to give the necessary time to the project will have more weight than the project manager's

Equally, if the team member spends too much time on the project, breaking agreements with the line manager, then the project manager must take steps to ensure that the situation is rectified or, when the cause is driven by the project's timescale, then the agreement of the line manager must be negotiated. If necessary, the project sponsor or other senior manager should be asked to arbitrate.

Sometimes, when full time team members are allocated to a project for many months (or even years), the project manager will be expected to assume the line manager's role in progress review and personal development matters with respect to the project work. Whether or not a project manager has official responsibility for the team members' personal development, any project manager who does not recognize the legitimate interests, objectives and perspectives of the project team will find greater difficulty obtaining the co-operation and respect of the team.

2. Why team building is important

If the project manager fails to build the team then he will lose a very valuable tool, probably the most powerful in the box. One of the great benefits of team working is peer pressure. People will strive harder not to let their team-mates down than they will not to let the organization down or their manager down. It is quite possible for individuals to work on the same project yet never feel part of a team. When extra effort is required it is often these people who delay the project. Of course, there are people you can always rely upon to give of their best and go that extra mile whether they are part of a team or not but you will be very lucky to get a team entirely composed of such people on every project.

Projects often make extra demands on people. They demand that people do extraordinary things. People will do the extra work and perform exceptionally for their team because of the social bond a team creates, particularly if the team is seen to be successful. People get hooked on success and will strive to maintain the team's reputation.

3. How to build the team

For smaller projects with small teams the start-up meeting
and project definition/planning exercise may be sufficient
initial team building exercise, particularly if it can be
combined with some humorous team exercises. This will be
especially true for organizations that regularly run projects.
The team will then forge close bonds during the planning
and implementation of the project.

For larger teams, especially where many of the team have
not met before, it is important for people to get to know
and trust each other. Away-days and weekend team
building functions are useful and rapid ways for people to
get to know each other. They do not necessarily have to be
the familiar 'outward-bound' type but must contain tasks
that stretch people intellectually and require team effort
for their solution. They must also be fun. It is a self evident
truism to say people who enjoy each other's company will
work well together. The 'outward-bound' course can be
great fun as long as nobody feels under pressure to
undertake tasks for which they have insufficient fitness or
which they believe will put them at risk.

4. Challenge or burden

Nobody will ever persuade me that jumping out of an aero
plane is fun and I have serious doubts about the wisdom of
abseiling down anything higher than 10 meters (30ft) high.
Likewise, I believe running up mountains is for the
seriously deranged so I leave those activities to those who
love them. The rest of us will do the organizing and be their
support crew. Remember, it is very important that leaders
should also serve and servers lead, in order for the team to
see both our strengths and those of our weaknesses we feel
comfortable revealing. There is a fine line between
challenge and burden. The most important thing to
remember is that when it stops being fun stop doing it.

This maxim applies equally to the project. A burdened team or team member is an ineffective team. Take some time out to review the project and the work. Maybe it is just that the team has lost focus. A half day break, followed by a re-focus session, may add clarity to priorities and work schedules. Redistributing the work, reprioritizing it or gaining agreement for a phase or project extension may be the answer. If the project sponsor is respected (unfortunately they aren't always) a review session with the team at regular intervals gives that extra reassurance that the direction of the project is correct and the work of the team is appreciated by senior managers.

Sometimes, bringing in a new team member (especially one with particular technical skills) will refresh the team but great care must be taken before taking this step because it can entirely alter the team dynamics. Gain the team members' agreement to the introduction of any new member and listen very carefully to any objections they may make. They have a large investment in the project and have a right to their say. Bringing in contract (temporary) staff poses less threat than permanent staff, especially if it is agreed that the contract will be terminated if the person does not show their worth in quick time.

5. Dealing with conflict

If you are unfortunate enough to have a clash of personalities there are several ways in which it may be resolved. Firstly, if the conflict is based on opinion and not merely behavioral, the team may be encouraged to say to the people concerned that they believe the conflict is unacceptable and that the individuals must settle their differences by arbitration. The arbitration may be that of the team or a higher technical authority. This is the ideal method because it reinforces the authority of the team as an entity and usually ends matters before they get out of hand.

If the conflict is one of personalities or is behaviorally based, then the project manager may have to speak to the persons individually at first and possibly together later. Sometimes behavioral problems are caused by anxiety about the work or the person's role. If someone is failing in their work or does not believe they can cope with the demands of the project, then attitude or behavior may be the first indicator.

The project manager must investigate the problem in a direct but sensitive manner, always allowing the person to have a face saving option unless this is totally impossible (very rare). Do not be confrontational. Spell out the problem in plain language and show how the behavior is affecting the project and ask for the individual's perspective about the situation. Listen and respond as positively as possible. People will sometimes act irrationally to situations. The addition of a positive perspective may be all that's required. However, the team member must understand that poor attitude and inappropriate behavior are not acceptable.

Sometimes the assistance of the individual's line manager should be sought in a friendly "off-the-record" way. The project manager will not want to damage the person's relationship with the line manager or be seen as questioning the line manager's wisdom in allocating the person to the project. The line manager may have the advantage of having known the person for many years and may shed valuable insight on the real causes of the problem.

If all else fails and a team member must formally disciplined and/or be removed from the project, the project manager must ensure that she or he has the agreement of the person's line manager, project sponsor, personnel officer (where applicable) and that all corporate disciplinary procedures are strictly adhered to. It isn't just that the matter may end in an industrial tribunal (which is a major consideration) but that all people have a right to be treated in accordance with due process, law and equity.

Question 12: RUP Project Plan

I am totally lost; I have to create a Project Plan using the Rational Unified Process. I know it has four phases; Inception, Elaboration, Construction and Transition. I have never used these phases. Where can I find an example of a project plan using RUP?

A: I don't have a sample SDP, or even a schedule, for a RUP-based project. It would really take a lot of writing to explain it to you.

The four phases (you named them correctly) have specific purposes. But they have in common the main *activities* of software development. The phases are distinguished not only by their purpose but by the relative amount of effort that is expected for each of the standard activities.

The basis of RUP is "Iterative" delivery. An iteration is a full swing through all of the standard software development activities, which results in an executable. Each iteration builds upon the previous by adding more functionality or quality attributes. Each iteration is a mini-waterfall.

Each RUP phase consists of one or more iterations. The activities of each iteration are:

Business modeling
Requirements
Analysis and design
Implementation
Test
Deployment

The supporting functions, like any other s/w development method, are:

Configuration management
Change management
Status and measurement management
Project management
Environment

Question 13: MSF project roles and responsibilities

Where can I find the roles and responsibilities of key individuals like the development team lead, development project lead, development manager, developer, project manager, QA lead, etc. within the MSF project methodology?

Can you give me a clearly defined responsibilities and roles for each position within each phase during envisioning, planning, developing, and stabilizing?

A: Roles and Responsibilities, in any methodology, are generally agreed between the parties. You may have a "starting point", the whole point of a Roles & Responsibilities exercise is to identify what roles are required, and what each role will take on as a responsibility. Remember as well, the difference between these two: One is doing, the other is ownership.

I would also keep in mind the difference between Accountable and Responsible, and make sure that the teams you are working with understand the difference.

Another consideration is that you have certain ROLES which need to be filled. Sometimes, a person can fill more than one role. I have, on smaller projects, been Project Leader, Data Modeler, and Testing Manager.

By the same token, sometimes a role requires more than one person to meet a deadline (two developers, or three testers).

Question 14: Gathering Business Requirements

I'm currently managing a group of application across various platforms/technologies (Java, COBOL, Db you name it) in a financial company.
I have to reverse-engineer these apps for extracting the functional requirements & business rules of the same? Is there any correct methodology /format I can follow while doing the same.

Going further I plan to construct test cases based on these extracted rules & requirements. Is it a good idea to build test cases on Business processes (the logical processes) or just the functional requirements of the application?

Also what is the exact difference & relationship between business requirements & functional requirements? Is it that business requirements are mostly logical processes whereas the functional requirements are the physical processes? Is there any site which gives a clear info on relationship between business requirements & functional requirements?

A1: Quote:
Is it a good idea to build test cases on Business processes (the logical processes) or just the functional requirements of the application?

I would do both. You want to make sure that the application meet the functional requirements, but you also want to make sure that they do what the users need them to.

When I'm working on writing specs for something, I like to sit with one or more users who are currently doing the task and see how they work and what they really need as opposed to what I think they need. The functional specs then become a collaborative effort to make sure that the users will get something that actually helps them do their job.

Unfortunately, many programmers don't make this kind of effort. So, you get software that meets the functional specs but doesn't actually help the user be more efficient.

The business requirements are usually stated in business terms while functional requirements are usually at a more technical level and may be unintelligible to the actual business user. Many companies have Business Analysts who work as go-betweens to ensure that the business requirements are accurately translated into system requirements via a Functional Specification or other similar technical document.

A2: There is a very big difference actually.

Business requirements justify why to develop so are like: What is the business problem being solved and how do we solve it: e.g. 'We need an ecommerce site for our soap product.' 'We need a tool for our inventory.' Why do we need the tool and what do we need it to do? For a developer it is too general a document to use for testing and developing.

Functional specifications are things like:
At login page, when the user enters a their user name and presses 'submit' they are taken to their account page; The logged-in header has the following... etc.

Don't confuse the function specs with the tech specs which are like: handlers, field names, changes to the code and table etc

Business requirements are written by marketers, PMs and execs for the IAs and designers; functional specifications written by IA's for the developers and testers. Tech specs are written by developers in order to work out and document the engineering on the site for communicating to current (other layer) developers and future developers.

Tech specs will be unclear to anyone but engineers, function specs should be clear to everyone.

If your issue is testing, I would start by working on function specs.

A3: I find UML is excellent for this task. However, to reverse engineer, you need to understand the forward engineering path.

Business requirements can be captured at three levels:

Global requirements go into 'Non-Functional Requirements Document'. A silly name, but it contains all the Business rules that affect everything that happens on the system. They are mostly used for security and availability requirements, but also make an excellent repository for things like 'Ergonomic Requirements'.

Operational Requirements, that correspond to 'Business Processes' and achieve one objective at one time on the computer session, map into Use Cases. There are lots of fancy definitions for these, but the 'one thing, one time at one place' is a good start. Then as people above had commented, these should only say 'What' people want to do and NEVER 'How'.
Business Rules. All the remaining Business rules should map onto classes or their associations. This assumes you

use classes. Often they are written in Business English, just as a list, but this is just a presentational approach.

In design, this data is used in different ways.

Use Cases tend to get used to identify one or more screens each. Sometimes, one screen may be used by several use cases.
The use Cases provide an excellent skeletal set of User Acceptance Tests. They identify all paths, all intents and what to look for when the use case terminates.
The key business classes should map fairly directly into the any relational database schema.
Finally there is the code.

To reverse engineer, you need to make use of these concepts:

Start with the screens and draw the menu structure. Most menu Items are indicative of a use case. Also look at the actions from the mouse keys, as they are NOT always reflected in the top level menus.

Look at the screens and try to imagine just what a user can do when working on that screen. Also note which other screens they have to use to do that thing. Maybe, you see a very complex set and the user could be working their way through a number of secondary use cases linked by <<includes>> and <<extends>>. Remember the 'One Thing' aspect of a use case. If they do a couple of things, look for a couple of use cases. Beware that 'a thing' in this context is NOT and action, but something that achieves an objective for the user; they could possible go get a cup of coffee after they have done it.

Look at the database schemas. These probably reflect the classes involved. The relationships then reflect fairly directly, some business rules like 'No more than three items at a time'. Data constraints are sometimes reflected here, like 'Must be over 16'.

You may be lucky and find an old copy of the 'Non-functional Requirements Document' as these have been used for centuries (Well nearly).

The code:
If you are lucky it is OO code, and you can find classes Components are sometimes Object based just by nature of the desire to encapsulate. Look for these.

If it is designed with Yourdon, then the functional units tend to deal with only a couple of data structures, each of which reflects a few classes.

Question 15: Splitting time between multiple projects

Any suggestions on how to split time between multiple projects effectively?

A: There is only one right answer to this question, Prioritization. How you go about that is the tricky part. In my experience, the best way to do this is to actually have your business partner prioritize, though for now that doesn't sound too possible. I would suggest weighing what will deliver the most "value" (sometimes value is in perception, so you have to gauge this one carefully).

Focus on the things that will enable making other things easier as well. Not all tasks have the ability to be made easier by certain things, but some do, so look for those. Don't let others put their monkey on your back either... this is how you really get bogged down, and lose valuable time during the day on the "Fire-fighting" instead of making real progress. I know this sounds vague, but so is my knowledge of what you are trying to juggle.

At the end of the day, don't be afraid to just say, "I'm going home" when you pass a "reasonable" hour. Sometimes resting yourself is the best thing you can do for your future productivity.

Question 16: Managing multiple projects

Our company has secured a maintenance contract for the client applications across different technologies, platforms. I have been asked to manage it.
The architecture is complex. In addition we are also busy with the daily support receiving calls from our users/clients.

Usually we handle 2-3 different work orders at a given time distributed amongst team members.

My problem is if we start working on say 3 different application/ work orders at the same time some new issue crops up and the priorities keep on changing.
This issue could be due to:

1. A user demand with a new urgent request
2. Limitations uncovered during the maintenance of the technology/architecture/environment (development or production)

This results in schedule slippage. Are there any best practices/ideas for managing a complex project with a high turnover of requests affecting the schedules of the current project?

Anybody worked on a project of similar complexity?

A: The really quick answer is a change management process. It's difficult to tell from your description where you are in the corporate "food chain" but it seems that you're not really in a position to push back by insisting on a signed off document by the project sponsors of all the affected projects.

If you were then you'd get the request, acknowledge it, do an assessment of the projects that are being affected and then send out a change management document to the project sponsor of the new project as well as to the project sponsors of the affected projects. Your assessment would show, for each project, the impact (delayed delivery, cost adjustments, etc.) and you would get the project sponsors to sign off on the change. Failure to get a complete set of signatures means that you change only the "signed off" projects (and that probably includes the new one) and the other(s) continue on their previously developed schedules.

Since you don't appear to be at that level, you are probably left with "the memo trail" solution: document for your boss (cc to the project sponsors - but I'd be politically careful about the distribution) about the impact. Yeah, I know: takes time and you don't have it. Make it. It's the only way you'll have to manage the stress you are currently experiencing.

You're likely going to get "compress the other schedules so everything gets done on time" memos. You handle those by confirming with the resources doing the delivery that the time estimates are accurate. After that, it's your own acumen that will help you negotiate the final results.

Incidentally, if you do get signatures approving changes then your position is significantly strengthened: when you get requests you can easily say "But Mary and Bob have already agreed to the existing schedule. Your change is going to have an impact on that. Perhaps you should discuss it with them first and have them tell me what changes they are prepared to accept in their schedules."

Some alternative random thoughts:

Even though you are swamped, there is still an opportunity to employ a formal methodology. It does *not* have to be all-encompassing -- you can restrict it to a single cover page with a bunch of items that need check marks and you can staple/paperclip appropriate documents to it.

Here are the "check mark" things I would have on it. Basically, each item below is a line on the cover page and never more than a page max of supporting info that you paperclip to the cover page.

"Charter" (deliberately in quotes): you don't want a fully fledged one, just one that names the principals (sponsor name, PMs name), budget, estimated work effort, internal priority (*your* priority, not the sponsor's), objective. You need this to keep track of scope changes. Scope creep rarely kills projects, but it does "kill" people because they keep getting asked to do more and more without any formal review/acknowledgement of the changes.

Schedule: Excel printout

Risk list: you need a focus on risk events that affect this project only. You don't need the traditional "staffing risk - might not have the right skill set at the right time", but you do need "Bob is going to get it started but then he's taking two weeks vacation" or "Customer facing app -- may need two or three recycles to get UI working smoothly". If this goes more than two paragraphs, you may be looking for too many generic risks.

Purchasing: you might not need in most cases to buy stuff, but keep it in just in case.

Staffing: "round up the usual suspects"; names and days of work only. You should also have a pre-determined "loaded cost" for your resource types so you can give a rough-and-ready cost.

Costing: now that you have a pre-determined cost rate for each resource type and a schedule you can quickly tell the sponsor what the project will cost the company. They'll still tell you to do it anyway (and you will) but it's a useful reality check.

Meeting Schedule: schedule for internal project progress (or lack of same!) meetings (you and the lead); schedule for external project review meetings (you and the sponsor -- and maybe some others). You're doing this to formalize the reviews so that they aren't ad hoc.

The info from these cover pages will help you develop your own metrics. These are for you to bring up during your annual salary discussions: number of projects you started, number finished, number still processing, total cost of all projects, total work days of all projects, ... anything that makes your workload look high and makes you look good. Anybody can quote numbers; with your cover pages you've got support.

Change management: one line per change to the project and each line has a page (or more, if necessary) describing the changes (mods to program specs, for example). Each line should show the change date, change id, change description (5 words), cost delta, time delta.

Note the low level of admin required on your part. One other thing I'd consider doing: getting a large whiteboard where you show current project status. You update it during the internal review meetings. It won't help you do your job but it will be a visible indicator to visitors about the work you and your staff are doing.

At the end of the day, the issue isn't a discussion of formal methodology (that game is finished and the teams have left the field -- you *need* the rigor and discipline that a methodology brings). The discussion is "how elaborate an implementation do you need". You need something you can put on a Palm Pilot -- just what I discussed above.

Question 17: Understanding OPM3

What is OPM3 ?

A: Whereas PMI's PMBOK is the de facto standard for managing individual projects, PMI's OPM3 standard provides a framework by which organizations can reexamine their pursuit of strategic objectives via best practices in organizational project management (OPM). OPM is the systematic management of projects, programs and portfolios in alignment with the achievement of strategic goals.

OPM3 simply provides a basis for examination of organizational project management; it is not prescriptive nor does it tell you what improvements to make or how to implement them. This is where the PMP qualified consultant can add true value assisting an organization adopt OPM3.

OPM3™ Organizational Project Management Maturity

OPM3 consists of three general elements. Knowledge which represents the contents of the OPM3 standard; Assessment which provides a method for comparing the standard against the organization's level of OPM maturity; Improvement identifies the changes that are required to improve the OPM maturity.

Organizations are increasing using project management to attain their business objectives, therefore project management needs to be aligned with overall business strategy. An organization's mission is translated into objectives which in turn get translated into strategies and tactics. Multiple initiatives are managed as a project portfolio (grouping of programs and/or projects) to facilitate better management of the work to meet the strategic objectives. OPM is the application of knowledge, skills, tools and techniques to organizational and project activities to achieve organizational objectives through projects.

The OPM3 maturity model illustrates the degree to which an organization practices organizational project management. There are two dimensions of OPM maturity. On the dimension of progressive stage of process improvement, you can identify where an organization's PM quality against the dimension of portfolio/program/project domains. Within these two domains lies the progression of incremental improvements in OPM maturity. Unlike other maturity models (like CMM), OPM3 does not provide an overall system of "levels" of maturity.

There are five steps. Prepare For Assessment entails understanding OPM and the OPM3 standard. Perform Assessment assesses the organization's OPM maturity, firstly at a high-level (existence of best practices), then at a detailed level (to identify which capabilities, associated with each best practice, are/are not demonstrated). The outcome of this step provides input to Plan for Improvements enabling the organization pursue improvements leading to increased maturity. Implement Improvements is where the changes take place and can be executed over a period of time. Repeat the Process is where you can either proceed to Step 2 to reassess the organization's PM maturity or proceed to step 3 planning the next phase of improvements. This emphasizes that OPM3 is not a once-off endeavor, rather a series of continuous assessments and improvements.

In conclusion, OPM maturity is described in the OPM3 standard through the existence of best practices, which is what industry considers being an optimal way to achieve a stated goal or objective. OPM3 includes basic processes for projects (contained in PMBOK), programs and portfolios domains, and are found in organizations practicing Project Management. Strategic objectives can be achieved more effectively by improving portfolio management. Improving portfolio management depends upon improvements in the project and program management domains. Therefore, increasing OPM maturity in each domain is of strategic importance.

Question 18: Problem juggling projects

I am a one-man IT department for a small company in Vermont. Though my title is IT Director, I do it all. I have a side project for one of our clients to do (a Flash feasibility study) and I was told that "all company work comes first." However, taking this advice realistically means that I will never get to the client's project. I recently made a list of my current projects (mostly database development and coding, debugging, etc for a web-based application we produced) and other ongoing IT duties (network maintenance, backups, etc). We are also setting up an offsite disaster recovery location with full redundancy and failover for our web apps and database. There is a lot to do.

In my attempt to get these projects organized, I input all of these projects into MS Project (it's what I have). I broke each project down in to sub-parts and linked them properly. However, right now the projects are in MS Project as if they were all going to be done concurrently. A few of them can wait until others are done but most of them need to be in work at the same time (e.g. one of our in-house programming projects AND the client's project AND the disaster recovery project). However, since I am the only resource available to be added to any of these projects, I am torn (no pun intended) on how to make sure that the projects get worked on simultaneously. Should I devote certain days of the week to certain projects? I already write Mondays off because of meetings and organization. If I go this route I have no idea how to code this into MS Project so I can give management a realistic view of my schedule. I would love to show them that there is too much work for me to do and give them a reason on paper to hire additional personnel.

Any advice is welcome.

A1: There is only 1 right answer to this question...
Prioritization. How you go about that is the tricky part. In
my experience, the best way to do this is to actually have
your business partner prioritize, though for now that
doesn't sound too possible. I would suggest weighing what
will deliver the most "value" (sometimes value is in
perception, so you have to gauge this one carefully).

Focus on the things that will enable making other things
easier as well. Not all tasks have the ability to be made
easier by certain things, but some do, so look for
those. Don't let others put their monkey on your back
either... this is how you really get bogged down, and lose
valuable time during the day on the "Fire-fighting" instead
of making real progress. I know this sounds vague, but so
is my knowledge of what you are trying to juggle.

At the end of the day, don't be afraid to just say, "I'm going
home" when you pass a "reasonable" hour. Sometimes
resting yourself is the best thing you can do for your future
productivity.

A2: My advice is this, take it back to simple project
management. You are going to have to be VERY STRONG
with your leadership.

Here are the keys:
Your company has a finite amount of the 3 following things:
    1) Time
    2) Funding (cost)
    3) Resources

You will have to be FIRM in your commitment to these
things. You have to illustrate to them that you can ONLY
do X amount in a given time frame. That if they want more
than that, they will have to expend Funding (increase costs)
to increase your resources. It is a triangle, and you can't

have 1 without the support of the other 2.

It is completely unrealistic for them to expect that you can deliver on these 3 items without some level of understanding. You can also equate the triangle this way:

1) Faster
2) Effective/Efficient
3) Low Cost

Again, you can not have 1 without the balance of the other 2. If you want high quality, you are NOT going to get that fast or cheap. If you want it cheap, it is not going to be fast or efficient... you get the idea.

Document
Management

Question 19: System Documentation

I'm working on a system documentation project and am in desperate need of a little help. The documentation is supposed to consist of network diagrams, various other diagrams, and then there are going to be sections detailing such things as back-up procedures, configurations, inv lists, etc. I'm trying to find some sort of a template or other resource to get me started on this project.

Do you have any ideas?

A1: Documentation should be based on the architecture, design, and specification documents you developed before beginning the actually build the project.

The functional specification or user requirements is probably the best template.

A2: You can, of course, seek advice from the overseeing bodies that "govern" such areas of interest as well in an attempt to gather templates.

IEEE, OWASP, various RFCs, etc. You can also try slipstreaming a bit by looking at presentations that universities and government PMs seem to post online to publish their efforts; I've found some interesting materials (and formats) laying about on the Internet from these sources.

Question 20: Records Management

What things would you do to improve a registry in government or can you give me an "Action Plan" for improvement of a registry in a government office?

What I mean by the term 'registry' is a government department which handles incoming correspondence and handles files of the respective organization department

A: To improve anything, measurement is needed. An excellent method of quantifying performance goals ("quality" goals) is Planguage by Tom Gilb (www.gilb.com).

Planguage statements have these parts (an example for your problem is below):
Tag - a unique persistent identifier
Gist - a short prose description of the goal to be achieved
Scale - a scale of measure on which to place goals
Meter - the method of determining where the project results lie on the scale
Must - a level on the scale; the minimum level to avoid failure
Wish - the far-end on the scale; the best, the ideal
Plan - a specific level to be achieved
Past - an historical benchmark.

An example Planguage statement for your problem

Responsiveness - the speed with which correspondence from constituents is handled.
Scale - calendar days taken to respond to a correspondence
Meter - difference between the date/time stamp on the incoming letter, as stamped by <who in the department does this> and the postmark on the outgoing letter

You must determine the following values, I'm just taking a guess

Past - [over past 5 years] average 35 days

Wish - 2 days
Must - 20 days

Plan - 10% improvement in average response time each quarter over next three years until average response time is 10 days or less.

Now that quantitative goals have been set [there may be other goals that you'd want to set] specific improvement initiatives can be designed. The degree to which each improvement initiative can affect the performance goal, Responsiveness, can be quantitatively assessed.

Question 21: Project Document Templates

My department (IS) is working on a project to create Project Management guidelines for internal use. We're trying to start simple (and hopefully keep it simple too), so are looking for simple templates for common documents - change control, RFPs, contracts, etc.

1) Templates for both packages and outsourced development.

2) Whole lifecycle, from Needs Analysis through Vendor/Product evaluation to End-user training.

3) These are IS-focused and controlled projects as the solution we are working on will always involve new hardware and/or software. In the past this dept has been mostly solution providers, but the role seems to be growing. I am new here and in my past experience I have generally worked with a larger scope. Perhaps we will have projects in which IS is not the largest component.

Any recommendation for a good source?

A: I had the experience of building a Project Office at a previous company. We created/adopted a number of templates. I should be able to supply you with a couple, though, I am new to tek-tips so I'll have to figure out how to e-mail them to you. Some guidelines though. Regardless of the project type, requirements, or anything else, there are certain things that I believe must be done.

1. Standard project plan format. For MS Project users this would be key header/footer information, standard Gantt table information.
2. Standard format/procedure for status reporting.
3. Standard format/procedure for risk analysis.
4. Standard format/mgmt process for project P&L.
5. Standard communication plan.
6. Standard change control format and reporting procedure.
7. Standard functional requirements doc format.
8. Standard deliverable acceptance document.
9. Written statement to client and stakeholders that ONLY the PM speaks for the project commitments. NO ONE ELSE.

While there will likely be others, those would seem to me to be necessary regardless of the project. I would also echo that www.gantthead.com has some good ones though I also do not have access to the premium site. I also want to put in a plug for Lotus Notes. We used it extensively as a repository for the project library and it was excellent. We also used it to develop some custom Project Office group collaboration tools. Alas, I could not take those with me.

Lastly, as I have told my teams, it is the documentation or methodology used; it is the diligence and attention to detail of the practitioners. It is critical that everybody on the team understand everything that can go wrong and what it could mean so that everyone works together to prevent problems. Led, of course, by a PM who knows what they are doing.

Question 22: Tips on Project Documentation

I have made an Exports Management System in Visual Basic 6 And Sql Server 7 as Back End. The project is ready & already implemented. Now I have to document the project, i.e. making a user manual, Software Documentation. I have very less idea about making documentations (never made any) & there is no senior's support. Can anybody provide me tips on making documentation for EMS? I just want info on what will be the topics in it? If u could send me a sample documentation of any other software, it will help me the most.

A1: Some ideas that you may wish to consider including in your documentation:

a) Describing the various menus that your system has, and what options they contain
b) Operating instructions to use the various options
c) A section on 'How to..' do such and such a task "e.g. How do I enter an Export Order into the system"; "How do I create a shipping schedule"; "How do I print Shipping documents"
d) maybe some 'FAQ's' Frequently Asked Questions would also be nice

The heart of most user manuals is really step-by-step instructions on how to do a particular task, and the sequence in which these must be done.

A2: I realize this thread is ancient, but I had to add a comment. The previous comment was based on an end-user software development model. If the actual software developed is, like many "quick" project developments, more fluid in design and operation, exception handling should have some place in the documentation.

This is not just error-trapping, which -if not done- should also be documented. "What do you do when". The type of situation I am thinking of occurs when you have multiple software options.

E.g. Software has Process 1 (P1), Process 2 (P2), and Process 3. Normally your sequence is P1, P2, P3, but maybe something changes, and you need to do P3, P1, P2 - AND this screws up your end result. You can spend a lot of programming time to address this, or you can document how to recover or work-around.

Project Software Management

Question 23: Software development process

What is Software development process?

A: A software development process is a structure imposed on the development of a software product. Synonyms include software life cycle and software process. There are several models for such processes, each describing approaches to a variety of tasks or activities that take place during the process.

Processes and meta-processes

A growing body of software development organizations implement process methodologies. Many of them are in the defense industry, which in the U.S. requires a 'Rating' based on 'Process models' to obtain contracts. ISO 12207 is a standard for describing the method of selecting, implementing and monitoring a lifecycle for a project.

The Capability Maturity Model (CMM) is one of the leading models. Independent assessments grade organizations on how well they follow their defined processes, not on the quality of those processes or the software produced. CMM is gradually replaced by CMM-I. ISO 9000 describes standards for formally organizing processes with documentation.

ISO 15504, also known as Software Process Improvement Capability Determination (SPICE), is a "framework for the assessment of software processes". The software process life cycle is also gaining wide usage. This standard is aimed at setting out a clear model for process comparison. SPICE is used much like CMM and CMMI. It models processes to manage, control, guide and monitor software development. This model is then used to measure what a development organization or project team actually does during software development. This information is analyzed to identify weaknesses and drive improvement. It also identifies strengths that can be continued or integrated into common practice for that organization or team.

Six Sigma is a methodology to manage process variations that uses data and statistical analysis to measure and improve a company's operational performance. It works by identifying and eliminating "defects" in manufacturing and service-related processes. The maximum permissible defects are 3.4 per million opportunities. However Six Sigma is manufacturing-oriented, not software development-oriented and needs further research to even apply to software development.

Process Activities/Steps
Software Engineering processes are composed of many activities, notably the following. They are considered sequential steps in the Waterfall process, but other processes may rearrange or combine them in different ways.

Conception
Establishing a business case for the development of the software.

Requirements Analysis
Extracting the requirements of a desired software product is the first task in creating it. While customers probably believe they know what the software is to do, it may require skill and experience in software engineering to recognize incomplete, ambiguous or contradictory requirements.

Specification
Specification is the task of precisely describing the software to be written, possibly in a mathematically rigorous way. In practice, most successful specifications are written to

understand and fine-tune applications that were already well-developed, although safety-critical software systems are often carefully specified prior to application development. Specifications are most important for external interfaces that must remain stable.

Software architecture
The architecture of a software system refers to an abstract representation of that system. Architecture is concerned with making sure the software system will meet the requirements of the product, as well as ensuring that future requirements can be addressed. The architecture step also addresses interfaces between the software system and other software products, as well as the underlying hardware or the host operating system.

Implementation (or Coding)
Reducing a design to code may be the most obvious part of the software engineering job, but it is not necessarily the largest portion.

Testing
Testing of parts of software, especially where code by two different engineers must work together, falls to the software engineer.

Documentation
An important (and often overlooked) task is documenting the internal design of software for the purpose of future maintenance and enhancement. Documentation is most important for external interfaces.

Software Training and Support

A large percentage of software projects fail because the developers fail to realize that it doesn't matter how much time and planning a development team puts into creating software if nobody in an organization ends up using it. People are occasionally resistant to change and avoid venturing into an unfamiliar area, so as a part of the deployment phase, its very important to have training classes for the most enthusiastic software users (build excitement and confidence), shifting the training towards the neutral users intermixed with the avid supporters, and finally incorporate the rest of the organization into adopting the new software. Users will have lots of questions and software problems which leads to the next phase of software.

Maintenance

Maintaining and enhancing software to cope with newly discovered problems or new requirements can take far more time than the initial development of the software. Not only may it be necessary to add code that does not fit the original design but just determining how software works at some point after it is completed may require significant effort by a software engineer. About ⅔ of all software engineering work is maintenance, but this statistic can be misleading. A small part of that is fixing bugs. Most maintenance is extending systems to do new things, which in many ways can be considered new work. In comparison, about ⅔ of all civil engineering, architecture, and construction work is maintenance in a similar way.

Process Models

A decades-long goal has been to find repeatable, predictable processes or methodologies that improve productivity and quality. Some try to systematize or formalize the seemingly unruly task of writing software. Others apply project management techniques to writing software. Without project management, software projects can easily be delivered late or over budget. With large numbers of software projects not meeting their expectations in terms of functionality, cost, or delivery schedule, effective project management is proving difficult.

Waterfall processes
The best-known and oldest process is the waterfall model, where developers (roughly) follow these steps in order. They state requirements, analyze them, design a solution approach, architect a software framework for that solution, develop code, test (perhaps unit tests then system tests), deploy, and maintain. After each step is finished, the process proceeds to the next step, just as builders don't revise the foundation of a house after the framing has been erected. If iteration is not included in the planning, the process has no provision for correcting errors in early steps (for example, in the requirements), so the entire (expensive) engineering process may be executed to the end, resulting in unusable or unneeded software features.

In old style (CMM) processes, architecture and design preceded coding, sometimes by separate people in a separate process step.

Iterative processes
Iterative development prescribes the construction of initially small but ever larger portions of a software project to help all those involved to uncover important issues early before problems or faulty assumptions can lead to disaster. Iterative processes are preferred by commercial developers because it allows a potential of reaching the design goals of a customer who does not know how to define what they want.

Agile software development processes are built on the foundation of iterative development. To that foundation they add a lighter, more people-centric viewpoint than traditional approaches. Agile processes use feedback, rather than planning, as their primary control mechanism. The feedback is driven by regular tests and releases of the evolving software.

Agile processes seem to be more efficient than older methodologies, using less programmer time to produce more functional, higher quality software, but have the drawback from a business perspective that they do not provide long-term planning capability. In essence, they say that they will provide the most bang for the buck, but won't say exactly when that bang will be.

Extreme Programming, XP, is the best-known agile process. In XP, the phases are carried out in extremely small (or "continuous") steps compared to the older, "batch" processes. The (intentionally incomplete) first pass through the steps might take a day or a week, rather than the months or years of each complete step in the Waterfall model. First, one writes automated tests, to provide concrete goals for development. Next is coding (by a pair of programmers), which is complete when all the tests pass, and the programmers can't think of any more tests that are needed. Design and architecture emerge out of refactoring, and come after coding. Design is done by the same people who do the coding. (Only the last feature - merging design and code - is common to all the other agile processes.) The incomplete but functional system is deployed or demonstrated for (some subset of) the users (at least one of which is on the development team). At this point, the practitioners start again on writing tests for the next most important part of the system.

While Iterative development approaches have their advantages, software architects are still faced with the challenge of creating a reliable foundation upon which to develop. Such a foundation often requires a fair amount of upfront analysis and prototyping to build a development model. The development model often relies upon specific design patterns and entity relationship diagrams (ERD). Without this upfront foundation, Iterative development can create long term challenges that are significant in terms of cost and quality.

Critics of iterative development approaches point out that these processes place what may be an unreasonable expectation upon the recipient of the software: that they must possess the skills and experience of a seasoned software developer. The approach can also be very expensive, akin to... "If you don't know what kind of house you want, let me build you one and see if you like it. If you don't, we'll tear it all down and start over." A large pile of building-materials, which are now scrap, can be the final result of such a lack of up-front discipline. The problem with this criticism is that the whole point of iterative programming is that you don't have to build the whole house before you get feedback from the recipient. Indeed, in a sense conventional programming places more of this burden on the recipient, as the requirements and planning phases take place entirely before the development begins, and testing only occurs after development is officially over.

Formal methods
Formal methods are mathematical approaches to solving software (and hardware) problems at the requirements, specification and design levels. Examples of formal methods include the B-Method, Petri nets, RAISE and VDM. Various formal specification notations are available, such as the Z notation. More generally, automata theory can be used to build up and validate application behavior by designing a system of finite state machines.

Finite state machine (FSM) based methodologies allow executable software specification and by-passing of conventional coding (see virtual finite state machine or event driven finite state machine).

Question 24: Measuring software development time

What is the best way to calculate software development time?

What is the best way to predict the duration from product requirements base lining to the acceptance of the product?

A1: Well, perhaps like many topics in project management, this question could have several answers.

"Time" could have two possible units of measure: Elapsed time ("duration") or Effort ("person-hours").

For duration, the most straightforward answer I can give is the time from the base-lining of the requirements for a product to the time when the product is accepted for use.

Different organizations use different terms for these milestones.

A2: Software cost/schedule is estimated best by using a model augmented by actual historical data from your own organization.

There are many software cost (and schedule) estimation tools; both freeware and commercial. These various tools are based on two main software cost models:
  (1) COCOMO (now COCOMO II)
  (2) Putnum-Norden-Rayleigh

Both these models are straightforward equations that you can implement in Excel. COCOMO has many more parameters (about 16) than PNR, which has only one super-parameter.

COCOMO is developed by Barry Boehm (pronounced "baaymm") at USC. You could download lots of information about COCOMO, including a freeware estimation tool, from his website at: http://sunset.usc.edu/cse/pub/tools/

Larry Putnum developed the SLIM estimation method. You can get his book "Measures For Excellence: Reliable Software On Time"

A really good freeware tool is Construx's Estimate, available from their website at: http://www.construx.com/

All these models (tools) in the same general method:

() Determine value of parameters related to projects at your own organization (different models have different parameters)

() Estimate the "volume" of the software product. There are many different methods of measuring volume but Lines of Code is used frequently.

() Determine the relative amount of code in the final product that is ...
  New
  Modified
  Reused
  COTS

() Determine constraints that are specific to this particular project that you're estimating. Such as

  Importance of meeting schedule
  Importance of meeting budget
  Importance of quality
  Peak staff

() Enter in the tool, get an answer.

Most importantly, however, these tools and their parameters must be calibrated to your own organization.

Question 25: Project Management Software

Why Project Management Software and what to Look for in Project Management Software

A: In today's world of international business, getting your project done on time and (preferably) under budget is paramount. You can't afford to take too long, or a competitor is going to beat you to the punch. Of course, time and resource management is a hot issue because of this, and many companies struggle to find that perfect balance.

Enter project management software: it's like a management consultant and an accountant rolled into one. Project management software not only keeps all your notes and information in one place, but also provides methods for everyone—from the general employee to the top executives—to keep track of task and project status.

Managing projects is an art: where project management software is your canvas, the tools it provides are your paints and brushes. The software should also allow you to easily match employees with specific skills to tasks that match those skills. The software should also let you track your project from the smallest task, up through the overall progress.

You need project management software that adequately covers your projects' needs, including collaboration features and easy-to-use and print reports. With software of this complexity, clear documentation is also necessary. Below are the criteria that TopTenREVIEWS used to evaluate project management software:

Feature Set – Project management software contain a lot of standard bells and whistles, including task and resource management tools and the ability to match resources to specific tasks and projects.

Ease of Use – Project management software features and instructions should be easy to find and simple enough for anyone to use, especially given the general complexity of the software.

Ease of Installation – The software should be easy to install and use, whether site-based or web-based.

Help/Support – Project management software should offer a comprehensive user guide and help system. The manufacturer should offer a customer service email address or telephone number so you can get answers directly from their technical support team.

Project Management – The processes, practices and specific activities needed to perform continuous and consistent evaluation, prioritization, budgeting and selection of investments. This provides the greatest value and contribution to the strategic interest of the organization.

Resource Management – A project management program should manage and control the limited resources needed to run a project, such as people, money, time and equipment.

Collaboration – The way that information and issues can be communicated—including email, conference calls,

meetings, intranets, web-based locations and so on—
should be simple and intuitive.

Whether you're a small business owner or an employee of a
multinational corporation, project management software
will streamline and simplify the process needed to get your
project done and out the door.

Question 26: Difference of Software Project Management from General IT Project Management

How does Software Project Management differ from General IT Project Management?

A: Actually, it doesn't. In 90% of IT projects, software makes up a large part of the effort. Next to, hardware, networks, and other infrastructure related components. So, in a sense IT project management has a broader scope.

However, the general techniques, outlines, and processes are the same. By focusing my course on software projects I can put emphasis on typical application software related issues, like user requirements, but that's all. If you are looking for an IT project management guide, I highly recommend my course.

Why is this basically the same?
I need to go a step back to explain this properly. Recent years a lot of complains about current project management practices have emerged. Methods are too rigid; too centralized in respect to planning, etc. (good examples of these methods are PMP and Prince 2) this even has resulted in a new breed of methods, agile a.k.a. light weight a.k.a. lean methods. Examples for project management are Last Planner (construction) and SCRUM (software development). However, the replacement of one normative method for project management by another may not me the answer to the problems projects are faced with. Different circumstances may require a different approach. If you need creativity to solve a problem or to create a design, you need an easy going, stimulating approach; if you are running towards a deadline to get in to production,

a rigid, centralized controlled environment is more the way to go. Depending on the environment and general circumstances a project manager should construct a process and organization that serves him or her best.

What make up the circumstances?
Without hesitation I would say "people". In my personal experience all major problems concerning projects are caused by human stuff. Intuitively I would state that the source of the trouble lies within the interest of the individuals and (the lack of) information/knowledge. As humans are controlled by their own fears and wishes, it's more then logical that if they are working under a project, they use the same mechanism. And it is just that this assumption that forms the basis of The Microwave Way to Software Project Management. See, the subject is software; the application area is very general.

Question 27: Choosing the right PM software

Can you give some tips in choosing the right project management software?

A: If you are thinking about using software to support your project management efforts, make sure you know exactly which goals you are pursuing. I'll give you seven to choose from to keep in mind when looking at software.

1. Improve project reporting and tracking
You "do" projects, fast moving and shooting from the hip; you get the job done. The planning is inside your head, you simply know you're halfway, and once in a while you send some vague spreadsheet to the financial guy. Your boss may want to use project management software to get a grip on you and your project, not just by "believing" in you but to get stone cold facts, to act when you're slipping.

2. Improve estimating and scheduling
To avoid history repeating itself over and over again, you may want to use software to retrieve historical data about your projects to improve your estimates and with that your schedules. Less embarrassment (being on time for a change) and more effective resource utilization.

3. Reduce cost or speed process up by automating workflows
Time is reported in different spreadsheets all over the company. First secretary collects them all. Second secretary maps them towards the spreadsheets with the schedules. Third secretary creates a summary management graph using another software package... Hmmm, must be a simpler, cheaper and faster, way.

4. Improve resource assignments

118

All those people running around; who's doing what? When are they available and can they do the job, do they have the skills? Making more effective use of your resources... sounds to good to be true. Can software do that?

5. Improve project communication

Having all the administration in a cigar box makes it easy to throw it away after the project is finished. Makes it problematic though for those who take over when you're ill or on a holiday. Yelling to the project team to get your message across works quite well when you're in the same room. Now try screaming across the Atlantic! There are of course more and more subtle issues around communication in your project that could get improved by using software.

6. Improve project team collaboration

It's great, just working from home in your bath robe; check in the "office" over the internet. Do some project work, do some sleeping. Wonder if bosses around the world are thinking if this "virtual office" thing is such a great idea.

7. Improve overall project process

Wouldn't it be great if a process was enforced, or better, encouraged in such a way, everybody has to? Just a great way to say "this is the workflow to be used". Sorry, have to use phrases like "continuous process improvement", "best practices", "quality models"... or just plain "my way". Isn't software great!

Question 28: Business requirements

The project that I'm working on is a very complex, large, and risky project. There is no strict PM discipline in the organization. There is no knowledge about SDLC. Business customers do not have full focus and "want" desire. They are continuing with the development on the existing systems. Instead of directing resources to new project, they are engaged in the legacy systems from IT and business side.

My difficulty is that how do I collect business requirements? Is it Business' responsibility to document business requirements or its responsibility? When I took charge for gathering business requirements, I did not do much elicitation since I'm the only resource. I had to assist in running those meetings, documenting, drawing some on the board, etc. I've moved to requirements validation part, so that I can know if the requirement documented is doable or not. This is a concept project. Nothing exists. Business customers are not cooperating. They now want to take over business requirements exercise starting documenting business requirements, flow charts, writing specifications, etc.

Can you help me how do I deal with this situation?

A: In the situation where "business" is the one that asks/needs the new system and "IT" is the delivering party, the requirements are the responsibility of the business, they are the owner of what they want, it is the way to communicate to the supplier what they expect/want.

This is a two-way street. As most businesses have difficulty in defining the requirements in such a way that IT can use them, it is most of the time a joint effort helping each other out. Just make sure that the business feels responsible for the requirements.

"This is a concept project. Nothing exists. Business customers are not cooperating." Well, that might be just the problem. Too abstract, too much on paper, not enough excitement. Try to find ways to make it alive. Discussions, whiteboards, videos, games, etc.

Question 29: Present Project Management Theory

What is Project Management Theory?

A1: There is no real single theory on which project management is based. When you look at the traditional (plan-driven, PMP, Prince2) approaches you will find a couple of theories that make up the foundation. Koskela and Howell (2002) provide us with four. They make a distinction between the theory of project and the theory of management. This posting is based upon their work.

Theory of project
Here the underlying theory is provided by the transformation view of operations. The idea behind this is that one can view the entire process as a sequence of transformations. Input is changed by an operation into a certain output. The project itself can therefore be considered as a sequence of related transformations. Underlying is the assumption that every larger transformation can be done in a couple of smaller transformation, creating a hierarchy of transformation steps.

Theory of management
Koskela and Howell make note of 3 management theories that can be found in current project management.

1. Management-as-planning
In this theory the management of an operation is done by creating plans. Management writes the plans, changes them if needed and implements them so the plans can be executed.

"This approach to management views a strong causal connection between the actions of management and outcomes of the organization."

2. Dispatch model
Management dispatches the work to the lower level hierarchies by issuing a statement that they should do a certain task. The communication in the dispatch level is one way, from the top down.

3. Thermostat model
This model is used to measure performance of the tasks. It is connected to the transformation view of a project. One has an expected (standard) output, and measures the actual output against the expected one. If a deviation occurs between the two, corrective measures are put into place to steer the process towards the expected outcomes.

A2: I want to share with you the following quotes:

"Laufer and Tucker (1987) find several troubling phenomena from planning in construction projects. First, the motivation for planning may come from outside sources: legal consideration and owner's requirement. Secondly, the primary internal motivation for planning is often control, rather than execution. Thirdly, the significance of control is corrupted by the separation of execution from planning, and in practice planning becomes a way of explaining, after the fact, what has happened. Thus there is almost total degeneration of the role of planning (Laufer & Tucker 1987): the role of planning is transformed from initiating and directing action before it takes place (as suggested by theory) to influencing and regulating operations while in progress (as intended in practice) and to follow-up and status reporting (as realized in practice)."

"Regarding the findings on planning, it comes not as a big surprise that a historically invariant observation on execution is that formal plans, if they exist, are often ignored."

"Control stimulates explanation rather than correction. Supervisors in most cases challenge the validity of the standard as a basis for control. They are distracted from today's and tomorrow's tasks in order to produce a historical record of yesterday's problems and a justification for what happened..."

"Control leads to manipulation of action... Managers may manipulate sequences to make the performance seem good."

"Control destroys the possibilities for collaboration. Increased monitoring at the activity level lead to greater pressure to assure its performance against budgets. This makes it more difficult to move resources between activities to improve project performance."

A3: In my opinion the core of problems within organization with a high political culture (better know as "who-to-blame" culture).

I once wrote: "how to ruin a perfectly good process? Give an order." With the highly educated people we have in the software business they have a strong wish of participation when it comes to determine what and how they should do things. Also for the time frame in which they should do things they have a strong opinion.

Not letting them participate in the "planning" stage reduces the commitment they have for the work to be done. Things like "not-inverted-here syndrome" and "if you think you know better..." will ruin the project. So Management-as-planning in combination of the pure dispatch model will be exactly the things not to do.

Also operating in a "who-to-blame" culture will have a

negative impact on the control structure. As planning / status reports will be used to provide a blame on some one, the planning will only be issued when one is 100% sure it will happen like that: so, actually after the fact has taken place. Or, more commonly, plans will hardly be used in reality; they will be written once at the beginning of the project... and that will be it.

Measuring someone's performance against a standard will trigger two options: either a discussion about the validity of the used standard, or people will just that whatever they have to match the standard, even if they know that it is not what is needed in the end.

So put standard project management models in a political organization, and you will have a ball.

A4: If the present underlying theories are not sufficient (or downright false) are there any theories that are correct?

Kosekela and Howell provide additional theories that in combination with the presented ones should solve the described problems...

"Regarding the theory of project, the (partial) models of operations as flow and value generation add the consideration of time, variability and customer to the conceptualization provided by the transformation model (Koskela 2000).

Similarly, the theoretical foundation of management has to be extended.

Regarding planning, the approach of management-as-organizing adds the idea of human activity as inherently situated (Johnston and Brennan 1996). Thus, planning should also focus on structuring the environment to contribute to purposeful acting.

Concerning managerial execution, the language/action perspective, originated by Winograd and Flores (1986), conceptualizes two-way communication and commitment, instead of the mere one-way communication of the classical communication theory.

The scientific experimentation model of control of Shewhart (Shewhart and Deming 1939) focuses on finding causes of deviations and acting on those causes, instead of only changing the performance level for achieving a predetermined goal in case of a deviation. The scientific experimentation model adds thus the aspect of learning to control."

Question 30: Software Management

How can a software management assure program success?

A: Between 40% and 60% of software failures and defects are the result of poor software management and requirements definition. In plain English, this means that about half of the problems encountered could have been avoided by making it clear, from the very beginning, what the customer expected from the respective project. This is to say that the programming was fine and the developers did their job well - only they did a different job from what they were supposed to.

The definition of a successful program is that it is 100% compliant with its initial requirements. But it those requirements contain mistakes, are unclear or poorly defined, then there is very little one can do to correct the problem later in the process. So, a bit of advance planning simply doubles the success changes of any software project.

The persons in charge with writing the requirements should be the project managers and the team in charge with software engineering, all the stakeholders, the clients and the end-users. Writing good requirements takes time and practice, and, even with all the new tools designed to help you, it will not happen overnight. You need a good, clear, organized mind, good programming knowledge (because you'll need to know exactly what your team of developers can do, and you need to make sure that you speak the same language with them) and, to a certain extent, good people skills. You will need to get in touch with the clients during this period, and to find out exactly what they want and how they want it. Some of them are not capable of explaining what they need, others don't have the time to meet you and look over the drafts, other thinks they know better and they give you all the wrong ideas and others will simply be very happy to approve your specifications without having a second look at them. You need to persuade all of them about the importance of this step, hold long, boring meeting, and then "translate" their needs for the programmers and developers. If customers or end-users are not available, despite your best efforts, you can use "surrogates" to simulate the actual users.

Make sure you remain in close contact with the client for the entire duration of the process. Their needs may change, or they may find out about something they forgot to tell you in the beginning - so inform them that you will always be available to meet with them and look at all the options again.

Also, the quality testing department needs to be informed about the requirements from the very beginning, because they will design their tests accordingly, and also they may have some details about what can go wrong in some cases.

One of the biggest issues is the time you have available for writing the requirements. Sometimes, when the deadline is very tight, the developers may start working before you completed the requirements, and this can cause a lot of problems later on.

The process of requirement management ends when the final product is shipped, and the customer is fully satisfied by it. However, the fewer modifications your requirements will suffer, the better for everybody. You should be able to trace your requirements all the time, and we'll have a look, later on, at the tools that enable you to do this.

In some cases, when a client comes up with an additional issue, it may be too late to change a requirement or ad a new one - the workload and the costs are simply too big to make it worth it. This remains subject to negotiation between you and the client - but your task is to know exactly what would be the effect of implementing new requirements, and to translate it into the language of the client (meaning that the client may not be receptive when he sees how many code lines need to be changed, but he may understand when you tell him how much this will cost).

Tracing requirements also involves additional tests, performed from time to time, to insure that the process runs smoothly and errors are identified and corrected early on. When faced with a big project, you may have different sets of requirements, some that apply to the entire project, and some for parts of it. When a certain design is implemented for a certain requirements, make a note about the effects and the alternatives - it may be useful for future projects (or even for the same project, if the client is not satisfied with the result).

So far, we've seen what software requirements are. In the following sections, we'll show some tips and tools about what good software requirements are. If this section is your responsibility, the wisest thing you can do is to get the IEEE Software Engineering Standards Collection. At 400 dollars, it may be somewhat expensive, but it will give you a lot of useful details about terminology, processes, the quality assurance and the user documentation needed. Also, the standards are conveniently given for each separate unit of the process - the specific part about software requirements specification is IEEE STD 830-1998, which describes the content of good requirements specifications and provides some useful samples. The guide is designed for in-house software, but it can be used for commercial software as well, with minor changes. Another useful reference is the "Standards Guidelines and Examples of System and Software Requirements Engineering" by M. Dorfman and R. Thayer, a compilation covering all the major standards (IEEE, ANSI, NASA and US Military). These are all flexible instruments, and should be used as such.

Question 31: Requirements engineering patterns

What is the importance of patterns in Software development?

A: If you've been around for a while, you've probably heard about patterns. As the name implies, patters help you cut time and costs by re-using the same solution, whenever the same problem occurs. So, a pattern identifies the problem and its context, and the best possible solution to it, in such terms that you can apply it again whenever necessary. In software design, patterns can be lines of actual code, but, more often, they are a textual description of the solution.

The pattern craze originates in 1977, in Christopher Alexander's "Pattern Language", and has continued since, with patterns used when they are necessary, and sometimes in excess, just to show off. A pattern language is the collection of the patterns used to address a bigger problem, such as, in our case, requirements management. All the stages necessary for solving a problem, as well as the actors, objects and tools necessary, are described in the respective process.

There are some tricky issues in using patterns. First of all, you have to identify them - which is done by analyzing the case model or the event response. When you have a pattern, you need to define it in such a way, as to allow instant recognition whenever you are faced with the same problem again. This is done by using several modeling methods, sometimes combined, in order to avoid the work of re-analyzing and re-defining a pattern, once you have already dealt with it.

Because they are not bits of code, but literary descriptions, the patterns are very flexible, and can be modified and adapted as the context of the problem requires. You should not think of a pattern as a solution to your problem, but rather as a step-by-step guide to solving the problem.

There are many good books out there that contain very useful, common patterns. You should start by reading some of them, until you are familiar with the concept, and able to identify at least some of the most common patterns.

"Design Patterns: Elements of reusable Object-Oriented Software" by Erich Gamma, Addison-Wesley, 1994 and "Object-Oriented Software Engineering - A Use Case Driven Approach" by Ivar Jacobson, Addison-Wesley, 1992, are two very useful books for object-oriented developers.

"Data Model Patterns - Conventions of Thought" by David Hay, Dorset House, 1995, provides a wider background, with solutions for different types of businesses.

Since the key to using patterns it to think abstractly, you'll need to do a bit of reading in order to familiarize yourself with the concept, and to understand how to make useful abstractions from a given problem. It will be a while before you can use patterns efficiently. In most cases, you will not be using the patterns created by other people, but your own, the ones you have been faced with before, because these are easier to remember and, probably, specific to your line of business. Usually, a pattern is considered as such when it has been used for at least three times to solve a similar problem. On the long run, patterns can save you a lot of time, but the main problem is that you are probably running a tight deadline and under a lot of pressure from the very beginning, and thus you don't have time to look which pattern should be used for which situation.

All patterns look a bit similar, even if they are literary texts. All of them have a name - if you are able to name them suggestively and consistently, you are more likely to find what you need quickly. They include a description of the problem, of the context, and of the intent (this is actually a sentence or two about what the pattern does). Then you have the so-called "forces" - which are a bit like guidelines for how to implement the solution. They help you keep everything in order and under control. Of course, you have the solution, since this is the whole point, and the resulting context, which describes the state of the system after the use of the pattern. You can also include examples and samples of where you've used the same pattern before, in order to make things clearer. Try to keep your document as short as possible - you don't want to read a short novel, when time is of the essence. A good method to identify when a pattern can be used is to match its name or any other of the above elements, to patterns already created (assuming you've named them correctly and consistently) and to check if you apply it to the given situation.

In writing software requirements, patterns are useful precisely because you don't have a lot of time to complete this stage. We've seen how important it is to prioritize your requirements, but this is a time consuming process. Sometimes it's a good idea to use a pattern to do this for you, in the same way as emails are prioritized according to different criteria. Another pattern available for the requirements is called Presentation, and it allows the display of data, when it is necessary to communicate it to human users. The Presentation pattern was created in order to allow you to focus on what data must be displayed, and not the method how to display it.
As you get more experienced in the use of patterns, you are sure to create some of your own, custom made for your specific needs and easy to identify and use whenever necessary. It may be a while before you can use patterns for their full benefits, but then you'll see it was worth the patience.

Question 32: Sequence diagram and class diagram

How would you relate sequence diagram from a class diagram?

A: Sequence diagrams express interactions among classes in terms of messages exchanged for a period of time, and, as we've seen, they fall in the category of interaction diagrams.
When you're done with the robustness analysis, you have defined most of your objects, their static relations and some of the dynamic relations. Now it's time to refine the diagram again, and to bring it closer to how the actual code will look like. Sequence diagrams can also be used to validate use cases.

You have four types of elements in a sequence diagram: objects, methods, messages and text. You will take the objects from the robustness analysis, and you can include their class, if you need to. The methods are shown as rectangles; while messages are arrows (messages are what stimulates an object to perform a certain action). Finally, the text comes directly from the use case.
This is the moment when you're most likely to get stuck, particularly if you've made mistakes so far. Make sure you allotted enough time to this stage to go back, if necessary. You will definitely need for attributes - check them out carefully, particularly if you plan to skip the class diagram and to move directly to the code after this.

When you draw the diagram, leave the methods last. You will need to check them with the controllers from the robustness analysis, but remember that one controller may translate into more than one method. Also, this is where you may decide that you can use some patterns already available, or that you can create some new ones that would be helpful.

As long as the use case diagram corresponds to the robustness analysis and the analysis corresponds to the sequence diagram, you are following your requirement specifications and will obtain what the client wanted. Otherwise, go back and see what you've done wrong. You cannot be sure that you've covered everything until you've drawn sequence diagrams for each use case, and then check the diagram with the text from the original use case, just to make sure that you didn't get "lost in translation".

Check your message carefully, and make sure that, for each of them, you understand which object is in control (and why, for all that matters). This is where you make some crucial decisions for your code - try to estimate how long a method takes, and if there isn't a shorter option available. Also, check the potential blocks or bottlenecks where your application will choke, and correct them at this stage. The sequence of the diagram is no longer an abstract drawing - this is what your code will also look like. Make sure you apply correctly all the principles of object-oriented design - you can't enforce them later on.

When everything was checked one hundred times, you can move on to the class diagram - which describes the types of objects and the relationships among them. It used to be called "object model", because this is exactly what it does - it models the class structure and content. This is the actual model of the code. All classes have names, attributes and operations, and the relations among them are the typical ones, such as inheritance, association, aggregation and containment. For complex classes, you can use a statechart diagram.

Question 33: Practical Software Requirements

What is practical software requirements?

A: When you agree that software requirements are necessary, make sure you understand what the word "requirement" means. If you ask ten people (starting with the developer and ending with the client), you will see that each of them understands something else. Make a quick note, this will give you an idea of one of the biggest problems you'll have to face: different people use the same words with different meanings.

Usually, the requirements are divided on several levels. The first level consists of the specific business requirements - business background and market needs, objectives, dependencies, scope and constraints. These are usually beyond the control of any stakeholder, but they should never be self-implied. They need to be discussed and detailed like all the rest, and included into a document usually referred to as the "Vision and scope document". This is the place to discuss the operating environment - something that will have a major impact on everything else. For instance, it the client plans to implement the software in China, it may be a good idea to find out now, since this will impact on every other aspect. Or, another example, if there will be many users and they will need different access and security levels, again, it may be better to plan in advance.

Now, when this is settled, it's time to discuss the user requirements. As said before, clients are not always very cooperative at this point, and it will be your job to convince them. Don't take for granted everything they say, insist on every single detail, and insist on talking directly to the final users of the program, or on getting information from them in one way or another. In the end, if something goes wrong, it will be your fault, since you can't blame the client.

Users will use all types of meaningless words, such the "the best", "the easiest", "user-friendly", "fully compatible with", and so on. It's your job to turn these into clear, measurable and traceable requirements. You cannot tell your client frankly that he won't get "the best" feature, but you can't tell the developer that he needs to "do his best", either. This is more or less similar to translating from one language to another. Fortunately, there are specific methods of doing so, and we'll look at them later.

You will turn the user specifications into functional requirements and quality requirements. Sometimes there's no need to bother with the difference between the two, but, in most cases, there is, because you'll need different measuring instruments once you start implementing them. Also, here you need to consider other external, non-functional requirements, which are not related to your client.

Now it's the time to turn all of these into software requirements specifications (SRS) and to hand them over to people who need to use them. It is vital to prioritize them - be realistic, some things may not be ready in time, others may not even to possible. Decide which requirements are absolutely necessary, which are necessary, but can be implemented later on (after making sure that everything else works, or even in a later version of the program), and which would be really useful to have, but, if the deadline is tight, may be skipped altogether. While you are doing this, check to see if there are some requirements that are not necessary at all - this happens more often than you may think. Sometimes the clients insist on functions they don't really need, in other cases you "assume" or "guess" what they need, and sometimes unnecessary requirements are leftovers from constraints that have disappeared or changed in the meantime. Make sure you can trace each requirement back to the constraint or function that generated it. If you think the client insists on an unnecessary requirement, check with your developers how long it takes to implement it, and then inform the client of the additional costs. Usually, when faced with the cost/usefulness ration, many people change their mind or review the situation more carefully.

Up to this point, you had to perform an appraisal for a program that did not exist; from this moment on, you will mainly need to evaluate what has already been created, to test and verify that the requirements were implemented correctly. Of course, you may still need to modify them or to ad new requirements when this is the case.

When something changes, make sure everybody is aware it, don't just inform the developer directly about what has changed. The entire team should have a strict set of rules, and all the changes should be written down for every stage affected. For every requirement document you write, make sure you also record, right on top, which version it is and when it was written/modified. Organized, efficient communication is vital. Also, this will prevent people from returning to mistakes which have already been eliminated by introducing a new requirement.

Make sure you check all the processes and instances affected by the new change. One of the worst things that can happen is to have a requirement implemented in one process, but ignored in all the other processes related to or deriving from the first one. For complex projects, it may be a good idea to organize a control board to approve or reject changes at regular intervals, and to make sure everybody is informed about the change and its status. There's no need of making it a very formal affair, or a very large board, as long as it does its job correctly.

Question 34: Stand alone project management software

I just read an article about Borland buying a project management software company to include in their own application life cycle tools.

I wondered, is there any future for stand alone project management applications to assist in software projects? I guess it would make more sense to integrate it as much as possible...

A:

1. I believe there will always be the need for stand alone software. It fills a market niche. It is used in organizations that are relatively new at managing projects. This is where they start walking before running. But as more projects get going in the pipeline, living in this stand alone world causes problems. Projects start slipping because of a lack of a project initiation/prioritization process and the inability to resource level across multiple projects.

2. These organizations will thrash around for a while trying to get a handle on all their projects and resources and ultimately look for a more enterprise type project management solution. So they mature and move away from the stand along environment. No worries though...other companies are just figuring out that they should get a better handle on their projects and start out on the bottom rung...with a stand alone tool.

This describes how things occur today, and probably will for quite some time. However, the process is all wrong. It is applying a "bottoms up" approach to project management. Organization should be taking more of a top down approach to project management. Ensuring that all projects align with the organizations strategic objectives, and will produce the desired rate of return. And that they have the man-power to deliver the projects in the targeted timeframe. If you believe this to be true, and are interested in a tool to support these Portfolio Management processes do a Google search for Portfolio Server.

I swear I am in no way affiliated with either Microsoft or UMT, but I just watched a demo of this product. This is where organizations should start! Simply get a handle on the RIGHT projects before you devote time and energy to trying to better manage all of them (including the wrong ones).

Question 35: Software Project

Why is software project management a poor
professionalism in the industry?
Why is software industry not different from other
industries?

A1: Well I guess it is not really a matter of software
project management but more a matter of the software
industry being relatively young. Metrics haven't really got
a change to mature so the models on which project
management should base itself are not quite accurate. I
mean, construction has a history of thousands of years.

So I think there lies the difference with other industries.
As human behavior has a large impact on software projects,
and the industry being young the models we have are not
quite accurate.

A2: If you are judging the quality of software project
management by the high percentage of failed software
projects, perhaps I can comment. KPMG Canada
undertook a very large survey of software project outcomes
in both public and private sectors in 1997. I used their
findings as part of my 2002 Masters Degree Thesis on
Success.

If I remember correctly, one of the main causes of failure
was the lack of project management for projects assessed
as being less than 1 man year to complete. Industry didn't
think such a small project deserved to be managed like
bigger ones....and so they failed. The bulk of projects
undertaken by number, lie under this 1 man year metric.
By starting a project and then largely ignoring its
management of resources, scope and quality, it is more
likely to fail than not. Obviously a small project does not

require a full management plan and team, but it reminds me of the saying "Fail to plan...plan to fail".

Question 36: Issue management Software

I currently work for a company that manufactures and sells scientific instruments. We have a team of service technicians across the country. These service technicians currently respond to issues at customers' labs that are reported to the sales person who sold the lab the instrument.

I am currently looking for a software package that our receptionist at the HQ can use to enter in issues with the customers products. That software will turn around and assign the issue to the appropriate service technician (based on State). That service technician is notified with email that a new trouble ticket has been assigned to them. The software also must be a CRM system built into so that the technician can get the name and address of the customer.

I'm hopefully become a web based so I am not hung out to dry with laptop issues.

Can you help?

A1: I've managed the implementation of HP's ServiceDesk s/w and this will do what you need and also be extensible for future requirements.

There is a web interface but the primary UI is not web based.

It's a fairly fully featured system and not the cheapest - but I don't have any hesitation in recommending it.

A2: I can assure that I'm not commercially involved at all. It happens that I have just worked with the sister product, which is probably one of the best wiki's around and have been managed by Jira.

This product is applicable to both topics, which are similar but different.

Try http://www.atlassian.com/software/jira/

Take some time playing with the demo, because it is very comprehensive and very flexible.

It is less obviously, directly applicable to the other topic, but is very effectively for project management. It differs from MSProject because it does not support any dependencies which is the basis of MSProject. Yet, MSProject is relatively weak on monitoring (IMHO). Hence I wanted the other topic not to dismiss it as irrelevant.

It is directly applicable to this topic, because it is Issue Management software. As it was appropriate to both topics and they were about different aspects of management, I felt it was right to include it in both.

A3: Take a look at www.maximizer.com!! Their Maximizer Enterprise version 9 is one of the best CRM products on the market today.

Question 37: Time estimate to write a program

My boss wants me to start giving him projections as to how much time it is going to take to write the programs he assigns to me.

How can I do this?

A1: Not knowing your skill level, or the complexity of the requested programs, I doubt anyone can help you with this problem. One thing to keep in mind though, when you estimate how long things are going to take, always base a "work day" on only 4 hours of actually work, not 8.

This reduction of time in the work day accounts for time wasted at lunch, in meetings, chatting by the coffee machine, etc. So, if in your mind you think to yourself, "I can do this in 3 days." You need to schedule 6 working days.

And, if you manage to finish ahead of schedule, it will only make you look that much better. It's better to pad your estimated completion times and have time left over, rather than scurrying around on the last day, trying to make a schedule.

A2: You can consider the following:

1. Language.
2. Your experience using that language.
3. Your experience with other languages.
4. Functionality of the program.
5. File access method (database, flat files, etc.)
6. Your experience using that access method.
7. Standalone program or part of a system.
8. Software Maturity level of your organization.

9. Availability of development and debug tools.
10. Your experience with those tools.

Whatever you do, do not fudge your estimate. Overestimating and coming in early shows you had no idea what you were doing.

A3: Being both a professional hard-core techie and a long-time project manager, I know the dilemma you are faced with.

The previous posts give you clues on what to do and what not to do. However, since you indicate that you do not know how to do the task, perhaps you are overlooking the obvious first-step.

Ask your manager for help. By way of the post, it is clear that you do not yet know estimating. As goofy as this may sound, your manager may not know either. Working together, you will likely find a common ground that will aid you both to better understand estimating and its requisite skills.

Other tips with your manager:

You may wish to explain that you (and others on your team) need help getting an estimating practice in place.

You may wish to identify a metrics collection practice (of previous efforts) is needed to accurately perform one art-form of estimating.

Question 38: Choosing software package

The family of my friend is in the textile manufacturing business, basically the work flow can be described as follows:

Concept / Original Design -> Sample Request -> Procure Material -> Sample Made (idea dropped, or changes made, or approved) -> Costing / Quotation -> Official PO -> Procure Material / Material Sent to Factories -> Production -> QC / Shipping Estimate -> Shipping Estimate Approved by Buyer -> Final QC / Packaging -> Shipping -> Invoice -> Payment

Pretty standard stuff really... Right now they're using a mix of Win98, 2K, NT, and XP, mostly just emailing and some Excel worksheets. Old quotations and POs are stored on paper and/or computer. They are looking for software that can keep track of current projects, as well as DBs that can store their material inventory, old sample info, quotations, POs, etc.

Any idea what their company can use?

A1: I don't know how big this company is and what their budget is for this but it would be great to create a system for them, using life-cycle principles like defined in Jackson System Development (JSD) to make a fully integrated system for them, of course using standard software where possible.

Perhaps you can advise them to hire a consultant whom will describe what is happening and whom can also make visible what information the people on all the levels need.

If the company is not very big, it is possible to create the whole system in COBOL in a PC-network environment which is very fast and efficient.

A2: After going through the details you have provided, the company needs software that can gel well with the Excel sheets that is being maintained by the company right now. I guess those Excel sheets may be having some data manipulating functions.

Well as you correctly pointed out, there will be a need for Database which will be required for storing the company specific information.
But apart from storing data, company requires to analyze the data stored in the database which may be the case in your friend's company too, though this is not clear from your description.

The type of database will depend upon the size of data being handled. For a medium sized data, the company can go far application (using MS office).More can be said if the requirements are made clear.

Question 39: Solution for Software Release Management

I am seeking for a more resolute approach to the release management process. Please enlighten me.

In my project we have 3 releases and 3 teams of at least 100 staff working on each release.

Currently Release 1 is in maintenance stage. Release 2 is in UAT and Release 3 is in build stage.

The problem is all 3 teams do not have the latest source code versions of each other. So there is this tedious code merging process where each code is merged line for line and it's done approx. ones in 3 months.

Than we do a UAT on this... and this cycle repeats endlessly. I feel this is an unprogressive approach and frustrating approach.

We cannot afford to have a single source control point because the will be more staff waiting for codes than working.

I hope you can suggest an approach which can perhaps throw some limelight into this problem.

A1: CVS is a very common open source project tool to maintain code.
As is "BitKeeper"...

Recommend you visit freshmeat.net
http://freshmeat.net/browse/52/

If you're doing Windows, M$ provides a source code

control package of their own.

In any rate, you need to get a software tool in place and use a "check out and check in" methodology for each release.

A2: CVS-like stuff is the best way to do this.

*It has the check in checkout features;
*You can track changing through tagging and email confirmations;

It also needs some serious Project Management with strong process.

*Are you tagging the code for each release?

*Do you have well regulated servers - 'this server for user testing only (Should have very same environment to the live server); this server for staging, this server for development) then migrating the code between each server for additional testing of database architecture updates between versions as you go through development.

I can't stress tagging enough!
karu76 (Programmer)
23 Mar 05 10:01
Hi guys, thank you for your advices. I will look into that CVS tool to study its advantages...

Yes planetant, we hv separate environments for the various stages. If we had adopted the one times release approach we could hv tightly coupled all the sources...

But since this releases are done in blocks and the blocks are interdependent on each other... this mess occurs...

Btw planetant, I don't understand the term tagging. Can you explain more?

I am thankful for all your suggestions...

L.Karu
planetant (IS/IT--Management)
23 Mar 05 11:10
Yeah, so this is the main thing to help you avoid trouble -
branching and tagging the code. I can't imagine
developing multiple lines of code from the same base
without it.

Still it needs a good PM or PE or even a QA director
coordinating. I seriously wouldn't worry about cost -
spend whatever it takes, 'cause with a little planning this
will save you so much dev time and chaos and worry and
employee turnover and QA time, etc.

Notice that you can even revert branches if something goes
horribly wrong:

Tagging and branching
The CVS repository for your project hosted on this site
supports branching and tagging your source files. At
certain points in your project, you may want to enable
development work in your project to progress in more than
one direction simultaneously. Instead of maintaining a
singular, linear path of development, CVS branching
provides a way to divert or split the source tree for ancillary
development activities without impacting progress of the
project's primary effort. Examples of reasons to branch
include:

To distinguish a clearly defined set of functionality in
project source files for QA and testing, or when you want to
try an experiment such as added features or functionality
without affecting the project's progress.
Tagging is included in the discussion about branching
because the two operations are used in conjunction.

Tagging allows you to "take a snapshot" of the overall project's state at a certain point in time, for example, to preserve a build with some particular characteristic. Because CVS manages individual file revisions, tagging is an important option for benchmarking the overall state of project source code. Files included in a tag will most likely be at different points in their respective revision numbering.

The critical difference between branching and tagging is the reason they are complimentary operations:

Branching affects individual files' revision numbering, whereas tagging assigns a common identifying marker across all project files at a fixed point in time.
So, for example, project files are often tagged at the point where branches are created.
Ultimately, branches in your project with successful outcomes get incorporated or merged back in to the main development trunk. When that happens -- and it may occur repeatedly on large or long-term projects -- identifying the point where this merge occurs is another reason to create a tag.

To tag project files, type:

cvs tag unique_tag_name
Your tag name can be a release name or date, a product version identifier, or whatever you choose.

To create a branch, type:

cvs tag -b unique_tag_name
Branching and tagging are complex topics with many considerations and options. You can find more comprehensive information and instructions in the following resources:

cvshome.org: "More about branching and tagging"
http://cvsbook.red-
bean.com/cvsbook.html#toc_An%20Overview%20of%20C
VS

"Marking A Moment In Time (Tags)"
"Branches" http://cvsbook.red-
bean.com/cvsbook.html#Branches

Question 40: Software Configuration Management

Can anybody explain what Software Configuration management is all about in layman's terms? I am a programmer pursuing a project management position and wanted to know what basically is the problem in the IT world that needs SCM in the first place?

A: Software Configuration Management is about being able to control and reproduce the environment in which your application is developed, tested, and deployed. It involves source control and a regimented process for promoting code from development to test and then production. It also involves documenting the other aspects of the environment such as Operating System version and patches applies, Database Version and patches applied, third party software versions and patches (modeling, ETL, reporting tools, for example), etc. It is most important when there are several versions of the software being worked on at once. One version in production, a different version in test, and another one or two in development. Sometimes the Test environment is subdivided into systems testing, integration testing, and acceptance testing. Just a basic intro. Let us know if you need more detail and I'm sure someone else will have a slightly different interpretation of what SCM means to them or in their organization.

The reasonable man adapts himself to the world. The unreasonable one persists in trying to adapt the world to himself. Therefore all progress depends on the unreasonable man. - George Bernard Shaw

Other Project
Management Issues

Question 41: Reporting/Data warehousing Task Management questions

I like to find a software (combined to a procedure) to manage a department projects AND tasks. By manage I mean the best repartition of tasks on resources, evaluation of time spent on tasks and projects, and weekly reporting.

Here are the situations:
- requirements come from other departments to provide data and reports, through a reporting client software ;
- sometimes requirements come by phone and we cannot avoid this (i.e. requirement from CEO!) ;
- most of people are working on long (annoying) projects ;
- some tasks are recurrent (monthly or weekly data loading, processing and check, reloading, re-processing when failure, etc.) ;
- sometimes the requirement is support or complain (wrong report, inconsistent data(!), webpage not working, etc.) i.e. the team does development, support, and maintenance.

We need to get a system to make the best scheduling possible for tasks. It is also necessary to make weekly reports on everyone's tasks for work assessment and compensation issues.

Can MS project be able to do all of that?

A: Yes, MS Project can do all that but I'm not convinced it's going to help you that much. Gantt chart approaches are best where there is a predictable sequence of predictable events, and as far as possible people are working on one thing at a time.

Your situation seems to be more like a supermarket checkout. You know the sorts of things that are going to happen but not the detail. You also need something quick and responsive. Re-doing a plan all the time is a rather boring exercise.

In the past, in this kind of development/support environment, I've just used a spreadsheet, and assigned time out in crude chunks. I also briefly tried to do plans for a group in this mixed role (because that's what they wanted) and you just find nothing ever goes to plan.

A2: I think you are talking about many different problems.

I would recommend you to try (if possible) to find trends in this kind of work.

In the issues submitting arena, the best solution is highly dependant on the kind of work you carry out in your organization and the culture. I am used to dealing with this kind of situation and I would recommend that you get senior management support to make mandatory the use of the system to submit issues. Make sure that you explain every user affected the problems you are facing and the benefits that submitting issues via the task management application will deliver.

Question 42: Meaning of Quality

What is the importance of quality?

A: Quality can refer to:

a. A specific characteristic of an object (the qualities of ice - i.e. its properties).
b. The achievement or excellence of an object (good quality ice - i.e. not of inferior grade).
c. The essence of an object (the quality of ice - i.e. "iceness").
d. The meaning of excellence itself.

The first meaning is technical, the second practical, the third artistic and the fourth metaphysical. All four meanings, and therefore the meaning of quality, are synonymous with good.

Philosophy and common sense tend to see quality as related either to subjective feelings or to objective facts. The subject-object in question might be a concrete and functional (e.g. Arisotelian) value to be learnt and applied (a and b), or a psychic (e.g. platonic) ideal to be apprehended and represented (c). A third view tends to see quality not as a secondary value that something has, rather a primary truth which comprises apparent subjects and objects (d).

So the quality of something depends on the criteria being applied to it. Something might be good because it is useful, because it is beautiful, or simply because it exists. Determining or finding quality therefore involves an understanding of use, beauty and existence - what is useful, what is beautiful and what exists.

In Business
Many different techniques and concepts have evolved to improve product or service quality, including SPC, Zero Defects, Six Sigma, quality circles, TQM, Quality Management Systems (ISO 9000 and others) and continuous improvement.
The meaning for the term quality has developed over time. Seven distinctive interpretations:

"degree to which a set of inherent characteristic fulfils requirements" as ISO 9000

"Conformance to specifications" (Phil Crosby in the 1980s). The difficulty with this is that the specifications may not be what the customer wants; Crosby treats this as a separate problem.

"Fitness for use" (Joseph M. Juran). Fitness is defined by the customer.

A two-dimensional model of quality (Noriaki Kano and others). The quality has two dimensions: "must-be quality" and "attractive quality". The former is near to the "fitness for use" and the latter is what the customer would love, but has not yet thought about. Supporters characterize this model more succinctly as: "Products and services that meet or exceed customers' expectations". One writer believes (without citation) that this is today the most used interpretation for the term quality.

"Value to some person" (Gerald M. Weinberg)
(W. Edwards Deming), "Costs go down and productivity goes up, as improvement of quality is accomplished by better management of design, engineering, testing and by improvement of processes. Better quality at lower price has a chance to capture a market. Cutting costs without improvement of quality is futile."

"Quality and the Required Style of Management" 1988 See http://www.deming.org/

"The loss a product imposes on society after it is shipped" (Genichi Taguchi). Taguchi's definition of quality is based on a more comprehensive view of the production system.

Energy quality, associated with both the energy engineering of industrial systems and the qualitative differences in the trophic levels of an ecosystem.

One key distinction to make is there are two common applications of the term Quality as form of activity or function within a business. One is Quality Assurance which is the "prevention of defects", such as the deployment of a Quality Management System and preventative activities like FMEA. The other is Quality Control which is the "detection of defects", most commonly associated with testing which takes place within a Quality Management System typically referred to as Verification and Validation. However, the American Society for Quality defines "quality" as "a subjective term for which each person has his or her own definition." Source: http://www.asq.org/glossary/q.html

In Engineering and Manufacturing
The Quality of a product or service refers to the perception of the degree to which the product or service meets the customer's expectations. Quality has no specific meaning unless related to a specific function and/or object. Quality is a perceptual, conditional and somewhat subjective attribute.

The dimensions of quality refer to the attributes that quality achieves in Operations Management
Quality supports dependability
Dependability supports Speed
Speed supports Flexibility
Flexibility supports Cost.

Quality <-> Dependability <-> Speed <-> Flexibility <-> Cost

In the manufacturing industry it is commonly stated that "Quality drives productivity". Improved productivity is a source of greater revenues, employment opportunities and technological advances.

Question 43: Migration Project

Currently I'm managing a migration project, migrating from older version of PB to the latest.

We estimated the migration time to be 6 months, but now it's getting delayed as we are in the 7th month.

There were some design flaws in the older version of the system, which resulted in errors. These errors were not prevalent in the older version (once in a month occurrence) and were rarely re-producible.
But now these bugs have become more prevalent in the newer/migrated version.
My question is who should be responsible for these?

We agreed with the client to fix the bugs caused due to migration (that goes without saying) and had made it clear that bugs not caused due to migration would not be fixed and the client had agreed to that.

My question is where do we draw the line and what approach should be adopted for these type of issues?

A1: A difficult problem that I have met before.

If it goes all 'legal', then you have significant problems. So my first thoughts are 'Talk to them'. That is probably so obvious, that you have already done it.

If not, collect your evidence in a form that they will understand; not that you understand, but they understand. Relate it clearly to the written agreement you have with them.

If it is as you say, then they will probably find funds to cover the extra costs.

If the increased sensitivity to this problem is due to your new architecture or you evidence is not 100%, then you may have to agree to share the costs.
If you are wrong, then the costs are yours.

The choice of these options will depend on how clearly you prepare the case. Of course, if you are in doubt, you may prefer to muddy the water, rather than clarify it.

I don't think there is ever a cut and dried set of rules for such cases.

A2: A few random thoughts.

(As an initial aside: I know you couldn't write a 10-page analysis of the situation for us but that means that any advice you get here may not be as germane as we could offer with additional background.)

The 7th month of a 6 month conversion is not particularly relevant. What's the forecast completion: next month? or late next year? If you've been keeping the client up to date with progress and writing change notices to reflect increasing knowledge about the conversion process then you and the client are already well down the road to a negotiated understanding of the rest of the project. Of course, if you haven't then that's an entirely different situation.

There aren't a lot of "size" numbers in your discussion. "Rarely" and "more prevalent" don't really provide sufficient information. There's also no sense of ranking for these errors: nuisances (columns on reports don't align nicely and sometimes a blank page appears in the middle of a report) or showstoppers (accounting ledgers don't balance at the end of the month; pay advice notices don't show proper tax deductions).

I'm presuming that you already have weekly status

meetings with the client and I'm assuming that the errors have some visibility within both organizations... I'd add a weekly triage meeting: the client brings the error list; a good-faith effort is made to allocate the list to "part of the conversion"/"not part of the conversion".

The "part of the conversion" list is triaged into "will fix immediately", "will fix at the end of the conversion", "will not fix". (This triage will let you focus on the main task: doing the conversion.)

The "not part of the conversion" errors are your company's revenue-enhancing (!) opportunities because of the additional (billable) work you will do.

My experience suggests that many errors will be handled this way and that only a few will be contentious. The triage meeting approach lets you deal with many items easily while escalating the contentious ones to more senior execs in both organizations.

There's one other sizing issue, too: your company and your client's company. If you're a smaller shop then the success/failure (profit/loss) of this contract may have a material impact on your company's future. In a larger consultancy, your organization may decide to throw resources at the problem to keep the client happy. If you client is large then they are likely a mature organization and may be well accustomed to situations like this and, equally, a much smaller organization might be more flexible and understanding but, simultaneously, not really unwilling but simply unable to pay for any remediation over and above the contractually agreed upon work.

Grooke (above) makes an *excellent* point: you have to explain things in terms they understand. Far, far, far too often, techie types think everyone speaks their language and sees the world their way. "The latest release's pre-insert trigger fails on a null secondary key where the key is defined as an alternate index" means absolutely nothing to a user or user executive.

It also only means that you've found a problem. You need to explain things so they understand it -- and you need to be able to follow through with "We have looked at this and here are two possible solutions ..."

Question 44: Removing specific dates from a project

I need to remove specific dates from my project. The tasks have a duration and the project is 31 days but it's for a proposal with no set timeframe as of yet. So I need to remove specific dates.

How can I do this?

A: You can do the following:

1. Tools | Options | View-tab.

Set the "Date format" to the last in the list which shows a day-of-the-week/week-number format

2. Project | Project information and set the start date to the first working day of January (it doesn't really matter which year).

3. Format | Timescale and set the Labels as appropriate.

Question 45: Performance Team Management

This is not for an actual working environment, I was just reading about this subject and felt that my source - although interesting - failed to provide quantitative answers to the following:

1. What methodology would you follow to identify the optimal profile of an arbitrary team? (be it a design team, development team, etc.)

2. How does the team profile break down into individual profiles: How would you go about identifying the optimal profiles of prospective team members - and should different team members fit different profiles?

3. If you feel that moving team members would help achieve your target team profile, but realize that this would interfere with established hierarchy, how do you achieve your goal without breaking moral?

It could be that there is a massive difference in team building, and team management, but I feel that my source did not expand on either: basically, it said to do stuff but didn't specify how.

A1: One thing to consider is whether you are interested in accomplish an objective in the shortest amount of time or whether the time can slide a little while you train your team to be better.

Why not ask each member what part of the project they would like to work on. Some may not be qualified for the areas they choose, but at least it lets you know where they would like their career to go in the future, and you can discuss that with them.

A2: I've always found the best team building exercise is to:

a. Treat your team with respect, expect the same from all team members.
b. Give them the tools and information they need to do their jobs, (Also keep them informed of things that may not directly affect them but which will make them feel disrespected if you don't tell them - an example is if you go to a meeting with a major customer, tell them about it even if it doesn't directly impact the project).
c. Don't play favorites.
d. Get rid of anyone who isn't a team player (you will have to try to counsel them first, but many of these people are unwilling to change).

A3: What type of budget?

The best activities I have enjoyed that accomplished these goals:

- Two or three day "camp" hosted by a company dedicated to your goals. Groups of you spend time trouble shooting problems (stacking tires on a 20 ft / 6 m pole), communication (production of plays to the group). This was by far the best ever. It cost money, but the objectives were met, and we maintained our "team" for years.

- Hire a sociologist/psychiatrist. Here, as comical relief, the person goes over personality types. This seems to be fun, but the underlying message is that it shows how watch can communicate with other personality types. A lot of fun, and really helped when dealing with people conflicts.

Less expensive things:

- Presentations by each department by various people on what they do. Although this helps people to get to know each other, the emphasis is on being comical. Have a theme. This week, the theme is the "Zoo", and the selected department has to make their presentations per the theme

- Lion tamer, chimp trainer. Some may be reluctant to "share".

- Visioning and direction planning. Including all allows all to buy in.

- Day-off vouchers for employee of the month, or by random draw. This does obtain your "team building" but money and time off are the two most desired rewards.

- Bowling for time off, or other rewards. You can get goofy
- most gutter balls, best flip.

Things to avoid:

- Too much alcohol can generate negative results especially if one or some are under a lot of stress and "release" too much. And are you liable if some one gets involved in an accident on the way home? Or inappropriate and unsolicited activity between the sexes. It would be counter productive if you got sued, or had to fire somebody during your team building exercises. If you drink, make sure it is safe and controlled.

- Non-family activity planned during family time.

Question 46: Outsourcing

What are other alternatives to on-site personnel recruitment?

A: "Offshore outsourcing helps the U.S. economy by lowering production costs for IT vendors and product costs for their customers and by helping to keep inflation low, according to a study released this week by the Information Technology Association of America (ITAA).

The economic benefits from offshore outsourcing will create more than 337,000 jobs by 2010, on top of jobs lost through outsourcing, according to the study, by economic analyst Global Insight Inc. ITAA called offshore outsourcing a "net positive for American workers and the U.S. economy."

(Quoted from Grant Gross
IDG News Service
November 2, 2005)

Businesses will continue farming out an increasing number of tasks to service providers in low-cost countries, with new countries joining that roster and existing ones expanding into more advanced functions.

To lower risk, companies are working more often with multiple vendors. The last year provided many examples of businesses moving away from massive, multiyear deals with a single service provider and instead being more selective about what they outsource to whom. ABN Amro last fall handed the bulk of its IT operations to five outsourcing vendors as part of more than $2 billion worth of contracts that involve 3,200 jobs. More buyers of outsourcing services are splitting tasks such as infrastructure management, application development, and help-desk services among a few well-chosen partners.

(Quoted from: Paul McDougall
InformationWeek
Jan 2, 2006 12:00 AM)

Question 47: Track IT and White Stone

What are the best tools out there to make sure that a small business firm keeps up with Help Desk Support, and Projects that we are working on a contract basis?

A: I have used Track IT, Universal Service Desk, among others. However, I reviewed a quite remarkable product called "White Stone" about 18 months ago, and for Incident Management/Problem Management, it was hands down the best thing I've seen in over a decade for this type of service. It also has great self-help, and self logging facilities. It is web based, but it is a very nice implementation, and seems very solid.
It certainly is worth a look, if you are in the market for a new tool.

Question 48: Project Management for a Tech Person

I have been working as a Network Engineer/administrator for 15 years. However I have had many jobs via contracting or working for vendors where I did what I would term Project Management. It appears PM is becoming or maybe has become a recognized need in SAP. Mostly I hear talk about PM on development/programming projects but what about other IT Infrastructure types of projects. That is my background. Network routers switches. Servers, load balancing, firewall etc. I would like to make a career move and get away from a purely technical role and use my technical knowledge as a step to doing more pure Project Management work.

How should I start this - with a certification? What is the market place looking for with respect to IT infrastructure type projects and PM?

A: PMI, Project Management Institute offers certification in PMP "pimp" Project Management Professional. There are also project managers in other industries, so the field is not narrowed to just IT.

Basically, a project is defined as a task that has a beginning and an end. The PMI tries to organize best practices of project management for a project within any field. IT certainly has its own qualities that need to be considered while doing project management, but the basics of PM can be applied.

Most important, first learn corp speak, i.e., instead of just saying "ok guys let's do x now and let's do it right", say: "in order to further implement our key strategic integrated solutions structure within a team-oriented paradigm hands-on approach on a global go-forward basis encompassing our corporate vision and core competencies with our key enablers with a fast-track deliverable, we will focus on our talking points in a highly motivated synergistic way while thinking outside the box with our value-added up-selling win/win philosophy and action item challenges within an emerging growth industry in order to leverage our major accounts with a highly focused impact initiative."

Question 49: Email - to - Fax Translation for Quotations

We are trying to move to paperless filing, but we currently use hardcopy/handwritten Material Requisitions(MR)'s that we send out via fax, then get back quotes, via fax and then send back the accepted/initiated quote for order. After all of this, it then goes to our accounting department where they cross check the invoices with the MR. Finally it is all filed in a large filing cabinet to be then stored off-site.

There is just too much paper transfer and the time it takes up to pull information among the tons of information we try to organize is extremely inefficient.

I want to design a template for writing our MRs faster and utilize Outlook to auto-send these MRs to our multiple vendors.

I think the first step is to figure out if Email-to-Fax and Fax-to-Email is even possible and someone has attempted this in conjunction with Outlook. Starting with an electronic document from the beginning is probably the best way.
We want to allow our quotations department and our accounting department to be able to easily send/receive/track/file and process.

Does anyone have any suggestions for solutions that have been used in the past for an Email-to-Fax & Fax-to-Email translation that is also organized and efficient and will work along with Outlook?

A: There's really only one solution in my opinion for what you are looking for, and that is Right Fax. Very robust, been around for years, and is used by many companies big and small. It's also reasonably priced.

It does integrate with Outlook, and does all the things you are talking about. The companies focus is on streamlining this kind of process.

Question 50: About "Changes"

How would you answer the following questions:

"Provide an analysis of changes made as the project progressed and lessons learned from the experience."?

What does it mean by "Changes"?

Does it mean: 'changes to the planned work activities'.

Or does it mean changes that occurred within the organization because of this project?

What "lessons" can be learned from such experience?

A: I would assume the question pertains to the changes to the project's triad of quality, cost, time. Every other change is immaterial as long as it does NOT affect the project.

Meanwhile, lessons are purely personal & subjective. As a start you can identify the failures, pitfalls, delays, conflicts encountered during and with the project and build lessons learned around these.

Your boss is referring specifically to the project, not to the impact on the organization.

As your project developed, there were variations from the original scope. Each of those variations is called a "change" and you use "change management" to document the changes to the project scope (i.e., the product deliverables) and the changes to the project deliverables (time, cost, quality). For each change you prepared a document that described the change to the project and got approvals for the change.

So the first thing your boss wants is a summary of that documentation. I'd put a single paragraph for each of the approved changes like a brief description of the change requested, date proposed, deltas on the date and cost, who approved it and when it was approved.

Question 51: Apply for PMP - Validate credentials

I just want to run my information by experienced professionals like you all so that I can be fairly certain that they won't reject my app - kind of paranoid of me, am trying to make sure I don't lose my $ 200 if they turn down my app.

I have an MBA degree and 6 years of experience as a Business Systems Analyst where I was involved with pretty much all software development projects from the concept to the delivery stage, and we used MS Project extensively to plan and track everything.

I have tallied my hours and so far I have narrowed down to 5 major projects in the past 4 years and they give me about 43 months with over 5000 hours.

About the contact hours course work - I took lot of courses on management in Grad school on Finance, Marketing, International Marketing, Management etc. But only 1 course that dealt directly with Processes and it was called Operations and Process Management. (36 Hours of class work)

I have taken 1 more course on using MS Project 2000 at a private learning institute, I also took 3 other courses were at learning tree - namely

Identifying User Requirements
Software Systems Analysis and Design
Relational Databases: Tools and Techniques

So from looking at these credentials do you guys think they meet PMI's requirements for both Experience and Education?

I also need some tips on how do I fill out the section that says "Your Role On Project" in the application in the miniscule space that the form provides. As the way I see it, that would have to delve in to some detail, what did you guys do?

A1: A couple of points:

The education contact hours have been satisfied by your courses but you might still want to think about taking one more course: a 35-hour PMP exam prep course. Almost everyone I know has told me that taking the PMP exam prep course was critical to their success. The exam prep course I took (and the sections I have taught) have been *highly* focused on a structured understanding of the PMBOK content.

When you get asked a question on the exam, you are not expected to answer the question but, instead, to answer it within the PMBOK context (initiate, plan, execute, control, close; knowledge areas; inputs, tools & techniques, outputs; definitions). Until you are comfortable enough to know that you can write out every process and identify it within the appropriate intersection of knowledge area and process group then you should not write the exam.

As for the submission of your application: you should be able to structure your answer showing how the work you did was at the intersection of one of the knowledge areas and one of the process groups. You will *not* be able to fill in all possible intersections (some are blank, btw) because it is unlikely that you will have worked in every one. The point is: you want to demonstrate your work was project and not process. You mentioned the roles you played. You could include that but the role name is not the work performed and it's the work performed that you are using to demonstrate that you have project experience.

A2: A final thought. Or, perhaps, more than one.

Your local PMI chapter should be able to point you to local PMP exam prep courses. Our chapter runs them semi-annually. We've done them ourselves and done them with a third-party organization. Both courses were as good as the instructors teaching them (which, if you read between the lines, say volumes).

I wouldn't worry about red flags. PMI does significant auditing of all submissions so even if you have one that doesn't raise a single red flag, you may still be asked to provide additional follow-up, supporting materials. In short: you're not being picked on, you're just being picked.

You probably already know this but ... Once you are inside the exam room with the permitted calculator, authorized notepaper and pen and you have signed on to the computer, take a deep breath because the exam clock hasn't started.

At that time, do your brain dump (processes, knowledge areas, equations, etc.). Take another deep breath. Read through your brain dump. Take another deep breath. Now you can start. When you start the exam and go to the first question, that's when the 4 hour clock starts counting down. Some do it in two hours, some take the full four. At the end of the day, nobody asks how long you took or what your mark is. They just ask if you have passed.

Don't try faking that you have passed, by the way. The PMI website has a location where anyone (or is it PMI members only?) can verify if you have earned the PMP designation.

Question 52: Tech language conversion

How do you describe in "tech talk" the Objectives, Key Deliverables and the Project outcome of a project you were involved in when you fill up a Job Application?

Sample Project Description:

Confirmed and documented complete system requirements by interviewing end users.

Tested and verified compliance with user requirements and other quality specifications during the course of development.

Created and managed an active project plan with a detailed WBS and deliverables schedule.

Provided weekly updates to team members on progress and briefed them on anticipated risks that could affect the project

Trained end users, client and deployed the system successfully and on-time.

A: Here's a sample:

Initiation – Defined Scope, Project risks, Assisted with developing Project charter and identified key stakeholders

Planning – Defined WBS and developed project requirements, constraints and assumptions

Execution – Flowcharted business processes for all 3 departments for user requirements, Tested and verified compliance with user requirements

Control – Measured project performance and ensured deliverables met approved QC standards

Closing – Obtained final acceptance, documented lessons learned, archived project data, created and distributed final project report.

Question 53: Difference between Project and Program

What is the difference between a project and a program?

A: Program: A group of related projects managed in a coordinated way to obtain benefits and control not available from managing them individually. Programs may include elements of related work outside the scope of the discrete projects in the program.

Project: A temporary endeavor undertaken to create a unique product, service or result.
I know of several clients who run Programs to manage projects that affect single, large applications.

In the case of something like SAP, you may or may not see interdependencies in projects.

In the case of large application with subprojects servicing multiple constituencies, it is appropriate that the Program exist to serve as coordination for the projects.

Thus I view Programs as a means of "PORTFOLIO" management. The projects within may be anywhere from totally unlinked to inexorably interlinked. However, the value in viewing the program is provided by having a point of focus for strategic consideration of investments, escalations, relative priorities, resource management, etc.

Obviously this method of thinking views Programs' function as very situational.

Question 54: Resource pool in Project

I want to do something very simple (I think) and basic to Project but it's not letting me.

I want to create a central resource pool which would be shared across projects. This pool would list employees and their specialties (technology, research, evaluation, etc). Projects would be attached to this pool. My vision is to have a separate file for this pool, into which updates would be added as appropriate. Sound reasonable? I thought so.

But when I try to implement this simple concept, mysterious things happen, such as the file contents disappearing on exit, the attached files' resource sheets not being updated, files turning into "read-only."

Can you help?

A: I've never heard before of any of those things happening.

Let's review the standard process.

1. Open a new, blank project.
2. View | Resource Sheet.
3. Enter resource data.
4. Save Resource Pool file and keep it open.

5. Open a project (new or existing)
6. Enter task information.
7. Tools | Resources | Share resources
8. Click on the radio button "Use resources" and choose the open Resource Pool
9. Assign resources

10. Save project file.

Some people have experienced significant performance issues when multiple projects using the resource pool are opened simultaneously. Others never experience the slowdown.

Question 55: When Boards Cross the Management/Policy Line

As I was reading this month's issue: "When Boards Cross the Management/Policy Line" I struggled with my organization's challenge. We are a very small organization (that does big work). We are currently financial and human resource challenged. The Board has been great about stepping up to the plate to assist in management issues. I'm thrilled at their level of commitment. My frustration now, is that the already blurry line is almost invisible. How do I let the Board into management when times are tough, and how do I reel them back in as times improve? Or how do I keep some sort of line? Help! Please? Thank you.

A: Tough issue--this takes some real maturity on the board's part, and some planning on yours. First, if you haven't already, develop a set of patter that goes something like this "thank you for doing that management work...I know that most board members don't have to do that much detail work, and I appreciate the temporary help. We'll get through this and then you can go back to doing the policy stuff we REALLY need from you."

Such dialogue puts you and them on regular notice that this is TEMPORARY.

Second, as you work out of your financial hole and generate budgets talk openly about your plan to get help and relieve the board of their management duties. Remind everyone that management should not be the board's burden.

Third, make sure you have board job descriptions that are policy, policy, policy. That way, when you do have the help and the board CAN go back to policy, you can nudge them based on their job description.

Finally, talk directly about this soon and often with your board leadership, hopefully your President if he/she sees the danger in this temporary situation. Make your position clear, and enlist his/her help.

Question 56: QMS (Quality Management System)

What do you mean by QMS (Quality Management System)?

A: A quality management system (QMS) is a system that outlines the policies and procedures necessary to improve and control the various processes that will ultimately lead to improved business performance. One of their purposes is quality control in manufacturing.

Although it may seem obvious that quality systems are necessary, many small or start-up companies function, or attempt to function, with only some areas covered. A survey performed in 1988 indicates the breadth of the systems established within the biopharmaceutical industry. The table below summarizes the systems and the percentages of the respondent companies that had established these systems. The age of the company and the industry had some effect on the extensiveness of the quality function activities. It is clear that testing is the primary emphasis. This supports the observation that testing or QC is perceived, at least in the beginning, as the emphasis of the quality function.

In manufacturing industries, statistical process control is a vitally important methodology used to control quality. This is important in the Six Sigma quality management scheme, pioneered by Motorola.

Concept of quality - historical background
The concept of quality evolved from inspection, measurement, and testing, which had been in practice for many, many years. Long ago, an artist or a sculptor took pride in his work and as a result always tried to excel in what was created. Mass production systems brought the concept of inspection by someone other than the craftsman in the first half of the 20th century.

Application of statistical control came later as a result of World War production methods. Quality management systems are the outgrowth of work done by W. Edwards Deming, a statistician, after whom the Deming Prize for quality is named.

Quality, as a profession and the managerial process associated with the quality function, was introduced during the second-half of the 20th century, and has evolved since then. No other profession has seen as many changes as the quality profession.

The quality profession grew from simple control, to engineering, to systems engineering. Quality control activities were predominant in the 1940s, 1950s, and 1960s. The 1970s were an era of quality engineering and the 1990s saw quality systems as an emerging field. Like medicine, accounting, and engineering, quality has achieved status as a recognized profession.

Current good manufacturing practice
According to current Good Manufacturing Practice (GMP), medical device manufacturers should use good judgment when developing their quality system and apply those sections of the Food and Drug Administration (FDA) Quality System (QS) Regulation that are applicable to their specific products and operations, 21 CFR 820.5 of the QS regulation. Operating within this flexibility, it is the responsibility of each manufacturer to establish requirements for each type or family of devices that will result in devices that are safe and effective, and to establish methods and procedures to design, produce, and distribute devices that meet the quality system requirements.

FDA has identified in the QS regulation the essential elements that a quality system shall embody for design, production and distribution, without prescribing specific ways to establish these elements. Because the QS regulation covers a broad spectrum of devices and production processes, it allows some leeway in the details of quality system elements. It is left to manufacturers to determine the necessity for, or extent of, some quality elements and to develop and implement specific procedures tailored to their particular processes and devices. For example, if it is impossible to mix up labels at a manufacturer because there is only one label to each product, then there is no necessity for the manufacturer to comply with all of the GMP requirements under device labeling.

Drug manufactures are regulated under a different section of the CFR: 21 CFR 211.

Question 57: Personnel Unaware of the Quality Policy

I have been writing up personnel unaware of the quality policy (they don't know what it is and have no idea where to locate it) as an OFI, should this be a non-conformity? Just wondering, I don't think my direct management would let me write it up as a Nonconformance anyway but I want to see what you folks think.

A1: It's not real important what you call it. 5.3(d) requires that "Top management shall ensure that the quality policy...is communicated and understood within the organization." If the ignorance you're referring to is widespread, it seems that "top management" bears the responsibility, and if you're going to be "writing up" anyone, it should be them.

Intellectuals solve problems; geniuses prevent them. — Albert Einstein

A2: How can you verify that management has ensured that policy is communicated and understood without asking people about it? It seems to me that if there's going to be a policy, and it's going to be considered a foundational element of an ISO quality system, and the standard (not to mention common sense) dictates that people know about it and understand it, there might be "value added."

Lies fly around the world while the truth is still putting its socks on. Mark Twain

A3: Ask your management if they know what the policy is and how it affects them in their individual work performance and how they personally help to achieve it.

They may stop sucking eggs and then allow you to do your work effectively.

What we learn to do, we learn by doing - Aristotle

A4: I have never been a stickler for "can you repeat, word for word, what the quality policy of your organization is?" Instead I usually ask is the quality policy for your company, can you tell me in your own words what that policy is, and what does the quality policy mean to you in your job. If you get similar answers about whether or not there is a policy and what it says, and people can tell you what it means to them chances are the policy has been communicated. So, if people cannot answer the questions, my guess is that the policy is not communicated and it is a nonconformance against upper management.

"It's fun to have fun, but you have to know how", Dr. Seuss

A5: This issue, however, is deeper than the simple act of asking people if they know the quality policy. If the goal is just to see if people read the policy and can provide some semi-coherent explanation of what it means to them, I agree that we can question the "value-added" aspect of wasting saliva in this dialogue.

IMO, the intent of establishing a policy is to ensure people understand that quality and customer satisfaction are very important priorities set by management.

To me, the appropriate time to ask anyone (and like Randy mentioned top management included) if they are "aware" of the quality policy, is when you (unintentionally) "catch" someone (intentionally) cutting corners, by-passing requirements or doing sub-standard work. That very moment they failed to abide by the quality policy.

It might sound mundane, but to recite or read a policy written on a poster, a badge, etc... is meaningless unless they truly understand what is meant. Like every thing else the proof is in the pudding.

A6: I assume you are performing internal audits. I would start as an observation. If the observation is not addressed by your next internal audit, I would elevate it to a minor. If you as an internal auditor do not catch this, an external auditor will.

Apart from requirement, I would think everyone needs to at least know what the quality system is about. A customer happen to ask an employee about the quality policy and they say "I don't know; who cares; not my problem " etc. is not the best advertisement. If enough effort went into the quality policy, everyone in the company should be proud of it.

A7: Regarding the thread topic (employees knowing the Quality Policy):
This is probably a case of an organization that creates a "highfaluting" Quality policy that serves "God, country, mom, apple pie, ecology, humanity, space aliens, etc." in turgid prose many of us would have difficulty reading out loud with a straight face and then sending the policy out to customers and auditors, but locking it and the Quality Manual up in the Quality Manager's office, never to see the light of day until the next desk audit by an outside auditor. If they do print it on a card for employees, the employees repeat it like a religious mantra in a long dead language with absolutely no real understanding of what it means. In point of fact, the guys who wrote it have no idea of what it means either, because it has no relationship to what the organization actually does.

Here is Motorola's. It says everything and nothing
Quote:

A8: Oh, this thread reminds me of my good old days. This was back in 1993, when we became one of the first 50 to be certified for ISO 9000 series in India.

The preparation for the certification audit was on. Everybody was **** scared of facing the D-day. The quality policy (Motorola type) was printed on small pocket size cards in three languages - English, Hindi and the local language. It was told to everybody that the first question that the auditor will ask on entering your work area will be "Tell me the quality policy". At the start of every shift, all workmen, janitors, security men...used to stand by their equipment and recite the policy word by word like taking an oath. This rigmarole took place in front of the auditors also. They were possibly so **** impressed that they never asked the question. God knows, possibly they never intended to ask.

Today, after two revisions of the standard, and after having completed over 300 certifications as a Lead auditor, I look back on that experience and cant help but to have a big hearty laugh.

Today I am neither an auditee nor an auditor (thank God!). As a consultant I sit down and finalize with my client his business plan first. This is an internal document of the management. Not pert of the QMS. Not auditable. This defines where the company is today and here it wants to be say 5 or 10 years from today. The quality policy comes next. This directs the efforts of the QMS towards achieving the business plan. And then come the quality objectives. These measure the progress of the company in meeting the quality policy directives (the business plan requirements). Now, the top management is interested in all employees being properly communicated about the quality policy. The policy is meaningful.

If you don't find the policy awareness amongst the

employees (what it means to them), its time to review the policy. Tell that to the management in whatever terms. If your message reaches, you have done your job as the internal auditor.

Question 58: Configuring MS Project

How to make MS Project show that Mondays are not available for project work?

A: You can follow the following steps:

1. Tools | Change working time
2. Click on the "new" button
3. In the popup change "Copy of Standard" to "XYZ Company", click the radio button next to "create a new base calendar", click on OK. "Create a new base calendar" was chosen because someone may have played with the Standard calendar and this way you can be certain you get a clean calendar.
4. In the pop up that shows the new calendar click on "M" (for Monday) to select all Mondays; click on the radio button "Non working time"; click OK
5. Project | Project Information.... in the popup change the calendar field to "XYZ Company" (or whatever you entered in step 3), click on OK.
6. View | Gantt
7. Right click on the Gantt chart and, in the popup, choose "Non-working time"
8. In the popup click on the radio button "In front of task bars", click on "Calendar" and choose "XYZ Company" (or whatever you chose in step 3).

You're done. Tasks will no longer be scheduled on Mondays.

Question 59: Defense Security Service (DSS)

Here is my assignment:

You are an IT Manager who has been placed in charge of implementing a DSS.
Lay out a plan for the next 2 years on how you will go about doing this.
Describe how you would work with others in the Organization.
Include a description of the human, technical, and financial resources you would need.
Describe anticipated challenges and strategies you would use to overcome these in order to implement the new system.

Can you provide a big picture view of how this plan will look?

A1: It's a catch question. Since you don't know what you're doing (typical situation) you can't budget or plan. Or at least not more than for the next 2-5 weeks. You need to know who wants the DSS, what they want it to give them (profit, market share, statutory returns...?) and how much therefore it is profitable to spend.

Seriously though, that is the sort of subject that people write 500 page books about. There's no simple answer.

A2: This is, presumably, a high school or university assignment question.

So: answer the question by defining your DSS. Once you've said what functionality you will support, everything falls into place. You next (and every succeeding step) is standard project management: define the deliverables (WBS), define the effort, define the tasks, schedule the tasks and predecessor/successor relationships, determine the resources you are going to assign to your project and assign them to the tasks. Fairly straight forward, actually.

Finally, prepare the risk mitigation and communications plans.

Remember, this isn't real life: it's an effort by your teacher to see what you're thinking -- or if you can think at all.

Look at your final mark, look at the marks for this assignment and budget your time and effort accordingly.

A3: Start by questioning everything you have been told and get it validated. For example, in the real world, I would be very suspicious of being asked to manage a two year (or longer) project without a lot more information on how and why the time frame had been estimated. Potentially long projects should be minimized where possible.

Anything you can't get an unambiguous answer for should be listed in your issues and assumptions log and circulated among the project stakeholders (probably your teacher and maybe the rest of your workgroup) for verification or repudiation.

A4: As we've said, in the real world this is a nonsense question (although many projects sadly do go like this). For an assignment simply refer back to the coursework preceding this task and incorporate the taught elements.

In your submission, emphasize to the marker that extensive review of the initiation phase issues (owners, purpose, success factors, business case etc etc) is far more important than the majority of the elements that form most structured methodologies (planning, risks/issues, quality etc).

A5: To begin with prepare a Word document for collecting knowledge of the existing system.

The document should list:
1. Existing system
2. Proposed system (be careful not to turn this in a detailed design document)
3. Brief architecture, interfaces, etc
4. Existing Business Processes
5. Existing Change Management & Quality Processes (and the processes you would propose)
6. Existing development methodology or the dev methodology/plan you would be following.
7. Current or Proposed Development, QA environments.
8. Stakeholders/ Users/Developers
9. Other interfacing/interacting systems

At the end of this document you should be having a clear picture of what you have in hand and where you are heading.

Question 60: Project Management for Maintenance Projects

I've been asked to manage a project by my company for our client and this includes maintenance & production support for existing 10 applications (which includes a plethora of technologies ranging from COBOL, PowerBuilder to Java/JXB) in the finance sector.

The applications as such are very much crucial and form the backbone for day-to-day business functions and there is no robust failover policy in place. The approach is mostly troubleshoot as you go. The client mgr is not willing to share production support with any other members of my team except a couple of us, whereas my contracting company mgrs would like to have production support distributed amongst all other members.

I see the client mgrs point very well (as prod support in too many hands has its own risk). How should I approach this specific situation?

A: First, this is NOT a project. This is a contract, a program, a support arrangement... This is NOT a project.

OK, now having done that, he's a little more insight. First, the Finance teams of every corporation I've been in have always had an insular attitude that borders on cases of paranoia. Perhaps, rightly so, especially in this world of Sarbanes Oxley compliance... Generally Finance doesn't like to play along with other IT strategies when it comes to their core systems, uptime, and support.

So what do you do? First, fully define what their expectations are for the "maintenance & production support for existing 10 applications". Start at a high level and get yourself to SLA-level terms: how rapid a response, what skills are needed, what Disaster Recovery obligations are they looking for? What kind of bug response they need? Backup and recovery: backup cycle, time to restore any particular dataset, offsite backup, restore point objective (how much data can be lost between now and what's available from the best available archive)?

Basically you need to spell out the requirements that they are going to require from a team. THEN, and ONLY THEN, can you begin to align your team's capabilities, skills, and projected expenses of providing the services to their original list.

You may find that your EXISTING team is capable of providing 80% of what the Customer needs; that leaves 20% to be negotiated over between additional cost for you to add skills/resources and them to reduce scope or slacken their SLA requirements.

You should also deliberately build in periodic (monthly) meetings with customer to discuss existing arrangements for support, performance, new/reduced scope, planned DR tests, planned restore tests, user training in readiness for DR events, costing relative to expected levels of service/hours used.

Finally, given your picture that you have a "small" team relative to a potentially wide base of required skills, many responsibilities, and DR commitments, you need to think through scenarios such as: your staff taking vacations, disaster scenarios that prevent workers from being available, disaster scenarios that prevent access to some or all networks/applications, people quitting service or being transferred, etc.

Question 61: Promotion interview tips

I have a Promotion job interview for the County I work for and one of the questions will be how I handle the following situation:

"If working on two high priority jobs and someone calls and wants a Third high project done right away and it is also high priority, how should the Project Manager handle it?"

I am thinking of answering this by saying I would Prioritize all the requests and delegate as needed or if by myself then analyze each customer need according to importance of the Department or consult with my upper management and advise them of each project.

Please advise.

A1: This question is doesn't have enough detail to be a practical question. I view it as a character testing question.

You should refer to PMI's code of ethics in talking about your approach. You should not compromise any work you've already agreed to take on. If any of the "bosses"/"customers" creates conflict for you between their interests, you should bring them into a room and require them to make the decision/agreements about which project(s) should be performed and in which order of priority using the available pool of resources.

You ARE NOT empowered to make the decisions due to lack of information, prioritization, cost/benefits analysis, etc.

Don't fall into the trap to describe how you'll do more

work. You want your answer to describe how you'll help the organization take a larger view of these competing interests. If the org. wants to get them all done and you don't have the bandwidth to work them at the same time, then there will be extra costs associated with staffing up from outside (perhaps).

A2: The first thing to consider is whether you have the resources to attack all three high priority items at once. If yes, then there is no problem.

If not, then you have a prioritization issue. You should be aware of the prioritization process and know what procedures to follow to arrive at the proper priorities. For instance, when I worked for the US Federal Government, the highest priority task was Payroll, or things payroll related. This was in writing. Sometimes, you might need to have a meeting with someone, perhaps even the president of the company. The worst case scenario is when you need to gather all three project sponsors in a room to have them negotiate the priorities. Don't forget to escalate decisions which you are not empowered to make. Those people get the big bucks for making those decisions and for making them stick.

A3: The question is *not* trying to find out how you will do the work.

The question is trying to see how you see project work. (Here's the context: project work is the allocation of scarce resources to accomplish the larger organization's mandate.) You need to turn the question back on the questioners by asking them all the questions necessary to determine the true impact, scope, priority, etc.

You should have at least a dozen questions to ask the questioners. It's so easy to ask close-ended questions (how many resources? what time frame?). You must make certain, however, to ask open-ended, higher level queries: tell me more about how this project fits into the department's goals; tell me more about why this project is being assigned to me.

At the end, you turn it back on them one more time. The questioners will have an agenda so, in a roundabout fashion, ask them for it: "I've addressed a number of immediately obvious areas; what other ones would you like me to address?" You'll likely get "oh, that's fine ..." Probe gently again "This sort of situation involves so many factors ... what are the most important ones to you?" And then listen very carefully to see if they mention anything outside of the framework you've already used.

Question 62: Dealing with bad attitude of project teammates

Does anyone have some advice on dealing with people's bad attitudes when working on a project in a team setting?

A1: Attitude is a symptom/reaction to another factor - generally. The reason for the attitude could be any of:

Poorly run project, poor compensation, insufficient oversight, too much oversight, incomplete requirements, too much work, lack of skills, overly skilled for the job, redundant work requests, conflicting priorities, bad weather....

You cannot legislate a good attitude. You can talk with the affected players, understand their concerns as best you can and attempt to take corrective action. If you find that their feedback is non-constructive you can indicate that your interest is to improve the overall team morale and that anyone who cannot contribute at a sufficient level of performance will likely be viewed for replacement on the team.

A2: There is a one day course I once attended called "How to work with Difficult People". My boss sent me to it because I had to work with another PM who was, uh, difficult. It was pretty cheap, under $100.

Then, several years later when I was a Director with a staff of 8 and had a Software Engineer who was a pain, I sent her to the course thinking it might work in reverse. It helped a little. She came back and told me, "we studied your type in class, you're a type C" or whatever.

When dealing with a bad attitude, the best solution is

"Root Cause Analysis" - determine what's causing the attitude and then, if determine if you can influence the cause.

You can't let one bad apple spoil the whole bunch. If you can't solve the problem, either remove that person from the team or request that they be reassigned and be prepared to back up your decision or request with your analysis.

The trouble with doing something right the first time is that noboby appreciates how difficult it was.
- Steven Wright

Question 63: Exit Strategy

I'm on my first IT PM job and I don't have an exit strategy! Hopefully this will not be required but can you give me any suggestions?

A1: Generally, you need to get customer acceptance of the project, closeout contracts, and then dismiss the project team.

The PMBOK has some pretty concise steps for this.

A2: Don't forget the Project Review, where you discuss what went right (plusses) and what could've been done better (deltas) during the project. This could be one meeting or several.

The trouble with doing something right the first time is that nobody appreciates how difficult it was.
- Steven Wright

A3: Exit strategy? That's a phrase often used to describe how you are going to extricate yourself from a mess.

Project closure? That's a phrase often used ... oh, wait, that's the same thing.

It's quite simple actually.

1. Did anything get contracted out to a third-party org? Make sure all contracted stuff has been done and verify who is responsible for warranty follow-ups after the project is finished but the work remains under warranty.

2. Financial. Nothing in depth. Just make certain there's a nice summary of budget and actual spending and, in a larger organization, make sure the project charge codes are shut down.

3. Staff. Do and be done. Do: Write up strengths, weaknesses and recommendations for each staff member (copy to the person, copy to the person's manager, copy to your manager and copy to HR). Be done: your manager has to do the same for you. By the way, if you don't like what your manager writes, you have every right to reply to the assessment. (And you can help your manager along if there's any delay in getting his/her assessment of you by writing it yourself and asking him/her to send it to you. It's a perfectly reasonable approach.)

4. Project Deliverable(s) acceptance: you need a signed letter from the project sponsor that the deliverables are accepted. It's okay to get a letter saying "accepted but ..." -- the critical thing is the "accepted" word.

5. Project Lessons learned: distribute copies to other PMs and your manager.

Question 64: How do you make a project moving?

I have been assigned a project in which I am the PM and the developer. My problem is getting the requirements and specs from the client. I have made repeated requests to no avail. What should I do?

A1: You can start coding immediately. You can always retrofit the requirements later.

Seriously, there is nothing you can do without requirements. Without requirements, anything you work on could be useless once requirements are known.

Who is the project sponsor? Make sure the project sponsor/stakeholder committee is aware that the project is on hold awaiting requirements.

A2: Discuss it with your supervisor. Then send an email (cc both your boss and theirs) and state that until a couple of meetings to determine the specs are held, this project will be on hold. Then drop it. Work on another project. This one will either go away or they'll hold meetings to get what you need. But DON'T do this without your supervisor's knowledge.

A3: The customer is personally ill-equipped to answer the question "what do you want me to build"?

I suggest ALSO putting together a framework of questions that help the customer figure out the areas of thinking that are not sufficiently nailed down for you to begin work. Try to use "dummy"-proof language to get the conversation started; you can geek-out once they get rolling.

Such as....

This application's purpose(s) is/are: [make them list]

This application's users is/are: [more list]

This application talks to these other applications: [produce list]

This application should be available to: internet web users, local building users, executives only, handheld users, telephone users, etc.

A4: What is right for you depends on your company's political and project management environment.

Who do you report to? How much authority do you have as PM? What is the PM methodology in use? How well does the business work with IT at your company? How rigid are standards with respect to functional specifications? What about budget, can you overrun if requirements are not well known as you converge on a solution using, say, a spiral development model? How visible is the project? Urgency? Importance? Etc.

A5: I have worked on a similar project and in a similar hostile environment.
Arrange a meeting (via Outlook) with the client reps. (if the client contact is hostile, include his/her boss in the meeting invitation and force them to respond.
Secondly have a questionnaire prepared off-hand to be circulated/discussed in the meeting. You may need to plan the questionnaire quite well in advance loading it with questions you want answered.

Also try to design the questionnaire in an objective format i.e. close-ended questions with one-liner answers

E.g.
1. How many sub-systems does the application have?
2. Names of systems?
3. No .of systems interacted with?
4. No of external interfaces?
5. Batch or client-server
6. How many batch? How many C/S?
7. Directory names etc..
Something like 50-60 questions (1 per min) should suffice in the initial meeting to get you started,
Rgds,

A6: I am in a similar situation: First time PM and Developer.

What I did was list a mass of questions to gather information for analysis. Such as: Business Logic, Marketing Strategy... and you know what: THEY DIDN'T HAVE A MARKETING STRATEGY!

To make matters worse, the Sponsor wants a stress-free life. I want to provide him with regular Project Updates, but he won't read them. I would like to see him involved in Scope Reviews, but chances are he will be out of the office - and he doesn't even carry a mobile phone!

Shoot. I'll just deliver him an appetizer and if he wants more, he will have to hire me again.

Question 65: PRINCE 2 Functionality

I am fairly new to PRINCE and starting to understand a few of the concepts involved.

Can someone describe what functionality of the PRINCE 2 management methodology is appropriate?

A: Whatever your organization wants.

1) Prince is a run-of-the-mill specification driven methodology. By itself it adds nothing to anything. The most massive IT cock-ups in the UK are usually Prince structured, so you might say it is good for raising project costs one-hundredfold and keeping your account manager very happy.

2) I've never been anywhere where they use it. Many places say they use it and may insist you are certified, but in practice they pay lip-service. Needless to say, the State organizations (i.e. Accenture, KPMG etc) are the worst offenders.

Having said that some of the basic products (e.g. PID) are reasonable templates, so you can use them. Just as long as you don't buy into the philosophy.

The idea you can specify everything up front, execute the project in pre-defined phases, base your testing on your specification etc is all very persuasive. If however you start to feel it's a little unreal - not the way the World works, don't worry. It's not you that's got the wrong end of the stick.

There are obviously many valid elements in Prince. The emphasis on products can often be relevant. The continuing referral to the original business case is wise, but it's really better to approach projects from a more valid standpoint.

Question 66: Planning Large Projects

I have been asked to come up with a project plan to
implement an IT system for decision Support.
I have to come up with the plan for the next 2 years,
resources I will need - financial, people etc. Milestones -
both long term and short term. How to manage
stakeholders.

Can you share your thoughts, any resources that I should
consult?

A1: Adelman's "Data Warehouse Project Management"
and "Impossible Data Warehouse Situations" are very good,
even if you are not going to build a DW, but some other
sort of Decision Support data store.

I would plan the project in phases, with each phase 3-6
months long. Do not commit to very much in the latter
phases as there will be lessons learned in the earlier phases
which will lengthen or shorten timelines in the latter
phases. Adelman's books along with your business
requirements will help you determine what belongs in
which phase.

A2: Here are a few pointers for you:

* see the big picture, then break things downs
* make it manageable
* keep it realistic
* ask
* use resources wisely
* SIMPLICITY is a good thing
* There's an overdependence on software, books, tech to do what people are trained and learn to do through life- M-A-N-A-G-E
* Navigate through politics, don't CUT your way through
* Plan to plan then do it, don't procrastinate
* of course you will take risks

Question 67: Project Management Dissertation

I am studying for a computer degree in the UK.
For my final year Project I have decided to undertake the design and implementation of a Project Management system.
As part of the development of this system I am required to gain knowledge about the factors involved in Project Management.

If it would be possible for anybody to answer these questions, or make available your email so I can direct these questions to you then I would be most grateful.

Questions: -

1. What would you describe your main roles and responsibilities are, as a Project Manager?

2. As a Software Project Manager, what do you find most of your time is spent doing?

3. What do you understand to be the key principle in Project Management?

4. Do you feel there are any personal traits in a Project Manager that would aid the successful completion of a Project? (outgoing, good communicator etc.?)

5. What software package(s) do you currently use to aid the successful management of a Project?

6. If you could improve on the software you use in any way, what would you do?

7. The number of Project Management Offices (PMO) in

the US & UK for managing Software products has increased by 54% in a single year. Do you think there is an actual increase in need for these PMO's, or is it a case of one PMO managing another?

8. As a Project Manager do you feel you need to have any technical knowledge of the product or service being developed by the Project? Would you be able to cope as well without it?

9. On a scale of 0 – 10 (10 always, 0 never) how many times would you say the Projects you manage/are involved in: -

A1: What would you describe your main roles and responsibilities are, as a Project Manager?

Recruit, build and motivate a team.

Accurately identify business requirements and build a solution that optimally meets those.

Guide subordinates - review their technical decisions etc

Manage suppliers - get good deals and optimal quality

Communicate and market the project to co-teams, management and the end customer.

2. As a Software Project Manager, what do you find most of your time is spent doing?

Business and Systems Analysis - talking to people about what things do, how they do it, how big, what's it for, who's involved etc.
Organizing and managing people

Communicating - meetings, reports etc that convey what the project is doing and how it is going

Reading emails, attending meetings to review how and whether events external to the project will affect the project.

Sizing and planning.

3. What do you understand to be the key principle in Project Management?

Management

4. Do you feel there are any personal traits in a Project Manager that would aid the successful completion of a Project? (outgoing, good communicator etc.?)

This is management and there are all sorts of successful managers. For IT, it is the key that you know a lot about IT otherwise you can't tell whether people are bullshitting.

5. What software package(s) do you currently use to aid the successful management of a Project?

Outlook
Word
Excel
Access
Photodraw
Powerpoint
MS Project

6. If you could improve on the software you use in any way, what would you do?

I can't think of anything I want. Once upon a time there were Case tools which sounded like they would help you but they never caught on.

7. The number of Project Management Offices (PMO) in the US & UK for managing Software products has

increased by 54% in a single year. Do you think there is an actual increase in need for these PMO's, or is it a case of one PMO managing another?

PMOs are for Management. They help Management see what is going on because project managers tend to be liars or delude themselves so nobody knows there's a problem until a major milestone is missed then all hell breaks loose.

8. As a Project Manager do you feel you need to have any technical knowledge of the product or service being developed by the Project? Would you be able to cope as well without it?

I don't need to know the specific product, business or project management methodology (except that it's the only way you get a job nowadays). I do however need to know a lot about all sorts of IT, business and methodologies to I can grasp the current one quickly.

9. On a scale of 0 – 10 (10 always, 0 never) how many times would you say the Projects you manage/are involved in: -

- Are on time
9
- Are on budget
9
- Fulfilled all requirements
9
- Experienced no problems
2

10. What do you feel are the main contributing factors to the failure of a project's capability to stay on time, on budget and fulfill all requirements?

Without doubt - the original

concept/technology/plan/budget was ridiculous.

People consistently underestimate the number of things they need to do and the propensity for things to go wrong.

People also love new or inappropriate technology when it delivers nothing but heartache.

The key to success is to continually revise the original vision as you move through the project and find things out. Don't hang on to previous decisions when you find there are better ones. Constantly keep thinking about the business requirement and try and out of your mind the technical solutions proposed.

Sadly as you can see, software packages can do little to help you on these key success factors.

A2: Here are my extensions to the above answers:

Qn. 1
Add: Manage schedules and budgets; Hand over the project; disband the project team.

Qn. 3
I would say management of a defined set of tasks and outcomes. (A project team is different to, say, a support team in that the project is supposed to come to an end).

Qn 4.
Many project managers can push a project over the line with little or no regard to quality or the welfare and cohesion of the project team. A truly successful project manager is one who can deliver a high quality outcome repeatedly with an energized team who have increased their skill base. I think the short answer is Leadership.

Qn 5.
I would replace Photodraw with Visio.

Qn 6.
A project website can be useful for large teams although it doesn't replace the need for face to face communication.

Qn 8.
I need to know enough to ask the right questions rather than have in-depth knowledge. Early in the project, I generally try and get the business representatives to walk the project team through the typical business cycle that is being automated. There are benefits for all parties in this.

Qn 9.
It depends to a large extent on the size and nature of the project and the amount of external pressure over which the manager has little if any influence. As an example, I was involved in a project a couple of years ago where a major external supplier had large slippages on their deliverables. Our team was ready on time but we couldn't deploy and hand over until the other parties were in place. Consequently, the project team could not be disbanded for a long time after the work was done. My team delivered on time, the global project was over a year late and we blew the budget keeping people around to put it into production.

Qn 10.
I entirely agree with these comments. I would also add: Under defined requirements; over-estimated benefits; incompetent senior management - including project managers (it is fairly easy to get rid of underperforming juniors on a project, very much harder to move a bad manager); and, of course, external forces.

A3: To deliver a quality product on time and within budget. To manage and allocate resources such that the objective can be obtained.

2. Requirements definition, redefinition, scope

management, change control, and squashing false expectations. (Requirements management).

3. Resource Management ($, time, people, supplies (computers, software, etc)).

4. The ability to foretell the future. Second best, the ability to predict the future. Thirdly, anticipate the future.

5. MS Project, Excel (task worksheets), Word (status reports), PowerPoint (briefings and status to executives), ERwin (data model) and BPwin (Business Process model).

6. MS Project definitely lacks a good resource leveling algorithm, mostly because it cannot interpret the skill levels of resources.

7. I am an IS consultant who has, in the past, and sometimes still, does PM. I have been in many organizations where there are Project Management oversight departments. Mostly they are helpful, but sometimes the PM office gets too caught up in the details of their paperwork and fails to see the real reason for the project.

8. I have been in both situations. I am not comfortable leading a project where I have no direct technical knowledge related to the project. I would not feel comfortable, for instance, running a project which called for the construction of a parking garage (a relatively simple construction project - no plumbing, for example).

9.
- Are on time 7
- Are on budget 9
- Fulfilled all requirements 9
- Experienced no problems 4

---

10. Misunderstood requirements, Incomplete technical specifications, Staff turnover, Over-optimistic task completion estimates, Poor assumptions and identification of risks.

A4: Here are my answers:

1. (a). Manage people resources (and, indirectly, the managers of those resources)
(b). Manage user expectations
(c). Manage a schedule
(d). Manage a budget
(e). Manage a plan (a plan is _so_ much more than just a schedule).

2. Managing people.

3. Rigorous change management processes.

4. People skills.

5. MS Project, email, word processor, spreadsheet, teleconferencing.

6. They all do 90% of what I want to do 90% of the time. Any increase in functionality would probably not bring a noticeable improvement in productivity.

7. It depends on the role filled by the PMO: gatekeeper or source of excellence and best practices.

8. No. But, for inexplicable reasons, specific knowledge is highly prized by project sponsors. A PM is a PM; an SME is an SME. A PM without SME knowledge will do a good job of managing a project; an SME without project knowledge will do a bad job of managing a project.

9. I'm in IT ... they are always over budget and late.

10. Senior management's refusal to accept upfront the estimates they are given.

Question 68: Daily responsibility of a PM in IT environment

I am at present a senior applications developer working for the financial sector. I am interested in PM and want to take up the exam. Because of the nature of my job I guess I would be suitable only as a PM in the IT industry. That's why I wanted to know the primary roles. If not the primary roles, what would any one be doing like for example in the role of an IT PM.

What is the primary day to day responsibility in general for a PM in an IT environment?

A: For one of the world's biggest banks I have a template for the responsibilities of a project manager. It goes on for two pages.

There is no primary responsibility, and what you do varies very much from project to project.

Accountable to the Project Board for delivery of the agreed solution for the project.
Ensure compliance with Corporate standards and demonstrate this by certifying that their project complies with Group Operating Model Principles, Policies, Architectures and Standards.
Ensure that team members are given the required facilities and that they are given the appropriate level of access to Group Technology resources and data. Access must be restricted to the minimum level for personnel to perform their functions on the project and must be revoked as soon as that reason is no longer valid.

Deliver the project in accordance with agreed functionality, time scales, budgets, policies and architectures.

Ensure a satisfactory relationship between all project contributors as delegated by the Project Board.

Establish effective relationships with business areas, setting up appropriate working groups where necessary.

Request the necessary resources via Resource Management and use the appropriate procedures for purchasing external goods or services.

Develop, publish, agree and maintain a project plan via the Planning process. This must include the overall project structure, reporting relationships, project deliverables, responsibilities, financial and resource requirements, acceptance procedures and standards to be followed. Identify and manage risks using prescribed procedures and tools.

Maintain control over issues and manage dependencies using prescribed procedures and tools.
Keep stakeholders informed of project progress by providing regular updates.

Ensure confidentiality agreements are maintained and adhere to all relevant legislation.

Collect information from stakeholders which may affect the running of the project, and action accordingly.

Ensure that the appropriate change management records are entered into the change tool and maintained accordingly.

Identify sign off / review points with other Group Technology departments and functions and ensure that they are achieved. Particularly those responsible for the take-on, support and operation of the deliverables produced by the project.

Monitor and control project progress and budget keeping firm control over changes. This includes ensuring that all costs are captured (including timesheet data) and that commitment or accrual accounting is practiced. Monitor commitments to ensure that the project is not jeopardized through lack of delivery of resources.

Provide regular project progress reports to the PCC (as per the frequency specified by the PCC) and any other governance authority.

Organize and train project teams including assisting Resource Management in arranging appropriate skills training for team members.

Ensure that an appropriate Documentation and Governance Model is used and properly applied. Ensure that the Configuration Management are informed.

Provide feedback to line management, as required, on staff assigned to the project for Appraisal and Development purposes.

Complete all close-down procedures relating to personnel, finance and resources and completes the End Project Report.

Question 69: Essentials of Project Management

What are the first things (steps) of note to someone just getting his foot in the door of Project management

How do I cope with several requirements - what software applications will help - How do I incorporate PM issues into my proposals - and business plans (I am starting a small business soon)

A1: If you are fresh to this, then read a good book. Don't go on a course. Most courses are just a structure for someone to rip you off on the pretext of some methodology or other.

Above all remember project management is primarily management - making people make something good happen. No software can solve this problem. The principle tools are Outlook, Word, Excel, PowerPoint and Access. Add in Microsoft Project and I think that's about all you'll ever need.

A2: I believe in the CMMI process. I do several projects a year and nothing else comes close. Read it and understand the principles. I'm not too crazy about the certifications. If the requirements are not fully defined, base-lined and the customer is willing to sign the bottom line, make requirements definition a part of the proposal. The last five years I've written several proposals in two parts. First: define and baseline the requirements/design, second: negotiate the work required to produce the product. PM is a part of the proposal, state it, cost and schedule. I've used several tools for tracking, mostly DOORS. You can accompli as BNPMike stated with a simple suite of to

231

overboard on high dollar software. Management is management, if there was a magic tool they wouldn't need us would they. Good luck on your business.

A3: It also helps to think of yourself as a resource manager. A project is usually limited by one of three resources. Money/budget, time/due date, quality thresholds/standards.

Quite simply:
Cheap + quick <> quality
Cheap + quality <> quick
Quality + quick <> cheap

A note from experience:
After the project is approved, make a record of EVERY change to the project scope or requirements, no matter how small it appears to be. Then estimate (over estimate) the time it takes to add this feature and ask the steering committee for the project for approval, denial, or deferral to the next stage.
Sometimes the grass is greener on the other side because there is more manure there - original.

A4: The world is dominated by formal, bureaucratic methodologies. These usually are 'waterfall' - define a solution and then proceed to build it in an ordered fashion. Preferably, delegate in as many prescriptive formats to as many sub-teams, most of whom don't have a clue about what the business need is, or even what the business is. Then have a load of testers and other innocents who are just floating in never-never land. Eventually your project will work (sort of) but in the meantime you will have blown away enough cash to save half the population of some drought-ridden African region. Sadly however, they die.

`lternatively, think in terms of dynamic (if unfashionable)
    `rnatives like RAD, Timeboxing, Extreme Project

Management etc. At least you'll feel there are few mortals out there that are sentient beings like you.

It's a distorted in which we live, but it's helpful if you can sit in that meeting thinking "I know you all think I'm daft, but actually it's you that are deluding yourselves..."

Question 70: PM Template

I am looking for a good template for managing projects and tasks. I have a diverse range of small community projects I manage and want a simple Excel template.

Can you help me?

A1: If you are at all concerned about project management then I'd recommend you don't use Excel. It's designed for fixed column spreadsheets i.e. things can't move about on the page. You'd be better of with Microsoft Project or a cheaper version e.g. Turboproject. These offer movable Gantt views.

In general each project is different so templates usually aren't very helpful. It's better to get used to thinking in terms of a Work Breakdown Structure. Think of all the things you need to deliver, what needs to be delivered in order to deliver them, and so on. Then build your plan around this pattern, adding the tasks that you need for each deliverable, its duration, who's going to do it and what dependencies there are between of all this.

The key to successful project management is not process or tools any more than fancy paint and canvas determined the quality of the works of Van Gogh.

Question 71: Advice on Test Plans and Stress Testing

I would appreciate any suggestions of free references or resource on creating formal test plans and planning stress testing in a multi-user environment.
Am developing a new project much larger than projects I had previously worked on.
My previous experiences have been on applications with maybe up to 5 end-users in one site.

My current project is for up to 25 users over 2 sites using a new database platform that I have little experience in.

My test plan will require considerable input from my customer with regards to upgrading some of their current software, creating test data and participation in stress testing so I am keen to document my requirements from them in addition to formal documentation of agreed benchmarks.

A: The basis for your testing should be your requirements. Based on the testing-V as described by Weigers in his requirements book, requirements are refined chronologically in the following order:

User Requirements
Functional Requirements
Architecture
Detail Design

Each of these design steps has a corresponding testing phase, which occurs in reverse order from the design.

Detail Design has Unit Testing.
Architecture involves Integration Testing.
Functional Requirements have System Testing or

Verification.
User Requirements have Acceptance Testing (or Validation).

Each of these testing phases should have its own testing environment, separate from each other. The objective of each testing environment is to control the scope of the requirements (new features) being tested. By limiting the variables being tested, it becomes easier to determine the location of an error and to repair. Hopefully, the error is not so severe that it becomes necessary to return to the design stage. However, if this becomes necessary, testing must return to the Unit Testing level, not at the testing phase where the error was detected, an often forgotten step which can introduce more problems.

Although Acceptance Testing requires the end users (as completion requires user signoff on their User Requirements document), strong Power Users and Subject Matter Experts should be available earlier in the testing process to create test cases, scenarios, and data.

Question 72: The difference between Project Description, Requirements, and Scope

What is the difference the following in a Project Description, Scope, and Requirements?

A1: Requirements are divided into two main parts, business requirements and technical requirements. Most of the focus is on business requirements. These are specifications and features that the users (business) has demanded from their new (or improved) system. Scope is a term which defines how many (and to what degree) the business requirements will be included in a particular portion of the project. For instance, across the total length of a project, all business requirements might be in scope, but for Phase 1 (or Stage 1), only the requirements related to CRM and ERP might be in scope. These would be specifically identified as being in scope, so that any changes brought to the table by the business could be labeled as scope change or postponed to another phase/stage of the project (and might be a scope change there).

To outline my response:

Project Scope:
Phase/Stage 1
1. (list)Business Requirements (specifications and features demanded from their new (or improved) system.
2. (list)Technical Requirements.

Should there be any changes:

Project Scope (slight different from the first Scope)
Phase/Stage 2

1. (list)Business Requirements (specifications and features demanded from their new (or improved) system.
2. (list)Technical Requirements.

If the scope change (if approved by the project sponsor), it would apply to the current stage/phase (stage phase 1 in this case, not 2). If the change was deferred to stage/phase 2, however, then this representation is correct.

The change in scope could be an addition, subtraction, or alteration in the way things are to be done.

Examples of technical requirements: You must run on Unix (or Oracle). It must be written in corporate approved forms interface (say, Business Objects). It must have response time of less than one second per query, etc.

A2: Scope is what is in, as distinct from what is outside of, your project.

The requirements are then related to what is in scope.

Description is a meaningless term.

Scope is a relative term. In a long project with many phases, there is scope associated with the entire project as well as scope with the phases. In addition, you can even think of scope at the individual project task level.

A3: If you're referring to product description, then this is simply descriptive documentation that will evolve as the product comes to life.

There's also scope definition which is breaking down the scope into manageable pieces. End result is typically a WBS.

SCOPE

Scope relates to the particular project's products and services, whether it's the creation of or enhancement of.

Keep in mind that there's product scope and project scope.

Product scope - the features and functions that characterize a product or service.

Project scope - the work that must be done to deliver a product with the specified features and functions.

REQUIREMENTS

Depending on what industry you're in, there are many types. In addition to the aforementioned requirements (i.e. business, technical), there could also be functional/non-functional, performance, design, etc...

As a rule of thumb, requirement should be written as a series of one-liners and only state WHAT needs to be done, not HOW it's done. For instance: The system shall provide a mechanism for a user to enter the customer's phone number.

Question 73: Types of outsourcing and how to stop outsourcing

What ways are there to outsource (offshore) and why should a company or companies not to outsource?

For example:

banks should never outsource because:

- safety
reasons:
experiences:

- quality
reasons:
experiences:

A1: Why not outsource? A company should readily admit that there are some business functions wherein they lack the needed expertise and this is one of the major reasons why there is outsourcing. Another reason is to minimize cost. Most companies look for cheaper labor costs and go to firms which offer highly effective and efficient workforce to support a business' struggling processes or functions. This is why most tech centers and software development companies are situated or based in 3rd world countries like India and the Philippines primarily to minimize cost. Another factor here is that these two countries can speak the English language fluently plus they both have able manpower who are highly educated in the IT industry. I'd like to stress out two factors again to end my post. 1st, outsourcing minimizes cost. 2nd, why not admit that some functions in a company aren't specialized by their head-count personnel.

A2: Your company could be "held hostage" by the outsource company. Not literally, but during the 1970's, bosses used to feel that they were being held hostage by IBM, since IBM really had not competition and could charge whatever they damn wanted. Once the outsource company gets your data, what will it take from an international legal perspective to enforce the contract?

Second point. Somewhat legal. In certain industries, there are requirements to handle certain personal information (banks, credit cards, health care) with a certain degree of diligence. Can you say that having that data in the hands of an organization probably exempt from US laws is a good thing? What would your customers and vendors think? Will the data actually be stored offshore? If not, how do you give the outsource vendor an adequate sample of data without trampling on privacy issues?

Communication issues; Communication costs - the cost for data and voice connections to the outsource location(s). Project control - might be difficult to control project management issues via telephone alone. Now you have the cost of visiting the outsource vendor or having them visit you. Is there a language difference between outsource vendor and client? Cultural issues - different holidays, perhaps even different philosophies on work ethics and quality, or what constitutes good service.

A3: OK, I used to work for a telecom-GSM company here in the Philippines. I was a system administrator for quite some time under the network quality department which specializes in putting up and optimizing cellular phone sites. In our pool, there were 12 contractual engineers who were outsourced from agency staffing/recruiting firms also situated in the Philippines. What these individuals did was survey possible cell site locations. They worked without benefits for short. Just the pay. They earned roughly 20,000.00 Philippine pesos or

$400.00 a month (which is a par amount of salary by Philippine standards). Everyday, they get exposed to hazards like, probable accidents (because they go to regions where there are rebel forces), microwave radiation (emitted by cell sites) and they don't get no travel and safety insurance, medical benefits and alike. That is one disadvantage. A company does save up a lot of money, but basically don't take care of their people, because come to think of it, those aren't their people at all. They were merely hired from staffing/recruitment companies. Of course those types of companies (I mean the staffing/recruiting) also don't want to spend on employee benefits. In a sense, they do give par to high salary for their employees to work for their clients, but don't actually take care of their people.

Another instance I should stress on is, that employees who are outsourced, don't feel at home with the company they're assigned to. They have this "bias" mindset that they have no favor from the management of the company they were assigned to.

Quality wise, at first, outsourced employees work hard. They work hard primarily to get the attention of their client company. Like "hello I'm here, I work hard, please make me a mainstay in this company" but when they've been working for years without getting absorbed by the client company, the Q-level starts going down. Instead of concentrating on the job they're supposed to do, they slack off and wait for their contracts to end. Especially when the client's management starts hiring headcount, preferring new entrants rather than absorbing them and the experience they garnered and familiarity with the company.

Touching on the tech-support-call-center phenomenon in India and the Philippines, all I see is a fast turn-around in recruitment. Here and India, (where time zones are like 12 hours ahead of the states) people have to adjust their sleeping habits to support the products of the west.

Because, usually, tech-call-centers perform support for the Americas and Europe. This poses an issue with sleep. Techs easily get tired because they sleep in the day, and stay up during the evening.

It would be frustrating. I'm glad I never applied for any outsourcing companies in the past. I had compatriots who did and were quick in jumping from job to job.

But I still feel that outsourcing is a need of companies now-a-days because of budget constraints and other reasons I mentioned in my first reply.

Question 74: PMP or other project mgmt goals

I'm a project manager at a small software shop. One of my goals for the quarter is to outline "professional objectives" - goals for improving my project management skills.

Offhand, the only measurable way to do this that I know is PMP certification. While I'm sure it's very valuable both for my company and me, I'm not sure about the time and $$ right now - company doesn't have a lot of cash to throw around and neither do I.

Any suggestions on other goal-setting from a project management perspective? Or those of you who have done the PMP process, if you think that is absolutely the way to go, I'd be interested in hearing that too.

A: Crawl. Walk. Run.
Year1. Year2. Year3.

Crawl: get the company to pay for your membership in PMI; download the PMBOK Guide and start attending local chapter meetings.

Walk: Pay for your own course to teach you how to pass the PMP.

Run: get the company to pay for the PMP exam (i.e., reimburse you if you are successful at passing it).

You may want to compress the time frame for year 2 and year 3 into a single year.

But, initially, just join PMI and learn what it's all about. You may decide that membership is all you (or your company) really need.

Many local chapters offer discounted rates for members to help them study. But it really depends on your personal study habits. You may be very self-motivated and the PMBOK and a couple of additional texts (Kerzner has a few, ESI has some good sample exams) could be enough. OTOH, you may learn best in a structured environment of a classroom.

I'm lazy and needed to attend a course to get me focused. The chapter's self-study course moved ahead in a well-defined plan and that helped me get started. We'd get a reading assignment (from PMBOK) for the next class. We'd be expected to read and understand and then the course would review the topic. Please note: PMI specifically forbids "teaching the exam" and all credible course providers follow that guideline.

If I were you ... I'd attend a local chapter meeting (they usually charge $5 or so extra for non-chapter members) and ask the people there for suggestions and guidelines. Most chapter meetings are attended by the executive (I'm at every one of ours) and they can direct you to some new PMPs and you can get info from them.

In other words: all roads are possible, you are the only one who can choose the road that is applicable to you and your learning styles.

Question 75: General tasks

I am looking for a way to add a general task, which can be done at any free time, even in multiple steps.

An example:
You have team member, scheduled and planned for about 80 % of the time for development tasks. On the other hand, you have a pile of documents that needs to be sorted. You want to schedule a task for the programmer to file the documents, whenever there is no other task planned for that person. (planning 80% on development, and 20% on the sorting task is not the solution I am looking for...)

Is there a way to spread that one task in MS Project 2000, whenever there is no other work planned for that person?

A: I've worked with MS Project planners on several occasions and they tend to shun automatic features. I now follow this style and find it is less stressful.

Build your plan based on the 80% tasks, review resource utilization levels and then add in your background tasks manually to bring utilization up to 100%.

You don't get Word to write your documents for you so why so you need to get MS Project to lay out your plans.

However, planning 80% on development and 20% on the sorting task is not the solution you are looking for seems like a rather willful position to take.

My view is if your week ever shows the slightest resemblance to any plan you made, then you urgently need to seek personality counseling.

My observations are

1) a plan is something that tests whether you can achieve what you want in the time you have to achieve it. Actually following a plan is a) extraordinarily hard work and b) achieves absolutely nothing. Manage day-by-day according to what seems good at the time. Re-do your plan only when you need to. You may need to because you've wondered too far away from what you originally decided or more often because some other person forces you to do a plan e.g. they're an IT Department Manager or QA Manager.

Of course millions of projects have people filling in detailed plans coupled with intricate earned-value calculations. These projects cost millions and 90% of the time are late.

When you write a detailed plan of what you're going to do at the weekend with your family, and follow it, then I'll consider changing my mind on the subject.

Sure I've done totally detailed plans and of course what happens is, well what happens is something completely different (because none of us is clairvoyant). So you spend another n hours correcting the plan and comparing it against the baseline. What a totally vacuous way to live!

2) A developer should surely be someone who doesn't need an analyst. I thought we got away from this model 20 years ago. Either sack all the people you've got or turn them into true analyst/programmers.

Question 76: Cost of charge to setup a small Network

I just started my own business and I've got a client that I've been doing business with for a bout 2 years. It's a Satellite Company and they just bought a new office and plan on moving in a few weeks. The office is a call center company and they receive calls and schedule the satellite installer to go out to the client's home. I will need to design and build a network from roundup. I will need to purchase all new equipment including a server, 5-10 workstations, a router (VPN capable), a few hubs, and software. I will have to run Cat-5 throughout the entire office to several rooms all leading in a central closet. Once the network is setup I will have to configure a Domain Controller and create accounts and join all the machines to the server. This is a pretty big job I think but I just don't know how to charge him. Should I charge per hour, entire project, or a contract? I do provide ongoing support by the hour. I've only been charging $30 an hour now that I've started my own business I'm definitely bringing up the rate to $80-$120. Has anyone done this and if you have how much did u charge and how did u charge the customer.

A1: I would charge on a time & material basis. Charge for your time at your rate and charge for all materials (plus a small handling fee 5-10%).

If you decide to negotiate a lump sum contract, you will need to be sure there is a detailed specification for the project of face the prospect of spinning your wheels as they (re)design on the fly.

If you do not have the capital to front for the materials, you can consider charging a down payment / retainer (possibly in lieu of the handling fee).

If they want receipts, make them pay for the materials themselves (directly).

Otherwise, you can itemize the charges for the materials on your invoice (just list what you are charging them, not what you paid).

A2: Assume the following:
Burden Labor Rate: 30%
Labor Rate Markup: 60%
Material Rate Markup: 40%
Misc. Material: 10% of identified material
Freight: 5% of identified material

1.   If your raw labor rate is $16.00 – your sell price would be $33.28 @ 37.5 % GPM
Labor cost: $20.80   sell: $33.28 @ 37.5 GPM
2.   Material cost is $100 (miscellaneous material cost: $10, freight cost: $5.50)
Material   cost: 100   sell:140.00 @28.6 % GPM
Miscellaneous Material   cost:10   sell:14.00 @28.6. % GPM
Freight   cost:5.50   sell:7.70 @28.6 % GPM
Tax (CA 7.75)   on sell   tax:11.94
3. Total cost $136.30   Total sell $206.92 @30.1% GPM.

Or a flat 35% GPM – Total sell: $222.53 (labor sell rate is $35.79/hr).

Stay in the 30-35% gross profit margin for financial success. Lower the rate to win strategic projects only.

A3: Definitely charge on a time and materials basis. If you charge a daily rate not an hourly rate then make sure you agree how many hours are in each day to.

Do a project plan with time estimates per task, roll it up to a bit higher level (unless the client wants to see every task). This way the client shouldn't get any nasty surprises (without a project plan you're basically asking them to sign a blank check to). Bear in mind something as simple as ordering a server can take an hour or more (including getting client sign-off on the spec. and cost etc).

Our rates depend on the level of consultant doing the work, it's about $200 an hour for a senior tech though (which is the level of someone that would do a project like this - apart from building the desktops/running cabling which would be a lower grade). Hardware margin is about 10% on list price - if you negotiate more than a 10% discount with the supplier though you should probably pass some of that saving onto the client.

I just can't stress enough though how important a task-level plan is though, it makes sure you don't overlook things, helps you budget the project and allows you to account for your time (assuming you update the plan with actual) - I don't know many clients that would be happy to pay an invoice for X number of hours without knowing what those hours were spent doing (you shouldn't have to account for every little task though).

A4: From the standpoint of a cabling vendor, does your state require and do you hold a contractor's license for installation of the cabling plant?

I would charge by the project, which would start by specifying what you will supply the client and at what cost. I would not break it down into X amount for a workstation and Y amount to configure it, but rather roll all the costs of ordering it, assembling it, configuring it, installing it, testing it, etc. together to give a price of $z per workstation.

A5: LIFE IS A PROJECT.

You should always charge in a per-project basis when deploying "solutions". I only charge in a per-hour basis when performing emergency technical support.

The only exception that comes to my mind could be when the client asks you to perform some task using specific parts supplied by him without your intervention and supervision. In that case you are just "moving boxes", and the only reasonable fee will be derived from your work and not from the device purchasing process.

Today, almost every well known brand can be easily found in the Internet by the client. But you will select, receive, handle, install, configure and give primary support to the devices involved in your project; so, a fee will be involved, and it should be natural for you and your client to deal with that. Just inform him about it and shut up!

If you have to make the planning, design and deployment of the whole system you should get paid for the engineering too (not only for the time spent running wires or installing software). If you break down the project price to every task to be performed, you will have to give him a "good" price (good from HIS point of view, of course), and it will be very hard to you to make a good profit for the engineering involved.
Again, if you are to handle the project from start to finish and from wiring to NOS configuration, THE ONLY REASONABLE WAY IS TO CHARGE IN A PER-PROJECT BASIS; NO EXEPTIONS.

Question 77: PM tool recommendation

I need to manage multiple (probably not more than 25) projects for a small business (i.e., limited funds available). I would like to assign resources to these projects and be able to check my company-wide resource utilization.

I do have MS Project, but it always drives me nuts! One thing I would like to do, that I think should be simple, is this: I have a task with a known starting date and a to-be-finished-by date. I have an estimate of the number of hours that each resource devoted to this task needs to expend. In MSP, I think that this is well nigh impossible to do.

Now, it could be that I do not know how to US MSP effectively, that is quite possible. If that is the case, if you would be kind enough to straighten me out, I'll stick with the devil I know.

However, if MSP cannot do this, can you recommend a tool that can?

A1: I recommend the following:

(A) You want to use Fixed Duration tasks.
1. Tools | Options | Schedule Tab: default task type should be Fixed Duration.

(B) It is easiest if you have already populated the resource sheet with the resources.
1. View | Resource sheet.
2. Enter all of your resources.

(C) Enter all your tasks.
1. View | Gantt Chart
2. Enter all of your tasks. Start, End, any other fields you

want. Do not assign resources at this point.

(D) Assign Resources.
1. Window | Split
2. In the lower pane, Right click and select Resource Work.
3. In the upper pane, click on a task.
4. In the lower pane, make certain "Effort Driven" is checked and make certain "Task Type" is fixed duration.
5. In the lower pane, choose the resource; in the Work column put the number of hours.
6. Repeat step 5 for each resource on the task.
7. In the upper pane, click once on the task to update the display of the resources.

If you want to change the date and keep the work the same then change the task type to "fixed work" and change the date.

If you want to keep the date and change the work then keep the task type as "fixed duration" and change the work for the resource(s).

A2: If you are using the MSP planning tool to manage multiple projects, I wish you luck. It is extremely cumbersome to use when trying to combine projects. You need an enterprise wide planning/tracking package. I think this would solve your dilemma. MS does have such a package but it is fairly new and I am not certain how stable it would be. I took a fairly extensive look at a tool that Niku has for enterprise planning. Pretty slick but can be a bit on the pricey side. Check it out.

Question 78: Applications Integration

I have been given a task to integrate the currently running applications in our corporate with surely doing amendments in all of the applications. We have 4 different applications running independently which do not communicate with each other at all. All of the applications have back end database 3 of them MS SQL server 2000 and one has oracle 8i. Now I need to know what approach and methods should I use to make all these applications running independently but communicating with each other and sharing info with each other which is necessary to have from each system. I have been reading some articles about ERP related methods but still a professional advice from professionals is always appreciated.

1 Service provisioning (In house developed)
This system was developed totally in asp with back end as sql server. All it does is covers the whole workflow of service provisioning covering all departments. Main info in this system goes is as:

customer profile, service info and other departments tasks.

2 Great Plains (Microsoft Product)
This system is used in Finance department for accounting purpose. Modules in it are out of the box solutions. Back end is sql server which is different from the service provisioning.

3 Remedy AR System (Remedy product)
This system is used by HelpDesk Department for trouble tickets for our customers, back end is Oracle 8i.

4 CRM (Bought package Web Interface)
This system as from the name is CRM used by sales only

and back end is Sql server again which is again on different system independently.

So the equation is

sqlserver + sqlserver + sqlserver + Oracle8i

In such different environment of applications and different back end databases how is it possible to make one common interface which is surely not a right answer isn't it ? my idea was that if we can make some common info available from each databases to each applications mainly customer info, services , invoices info, installations. We are and ISP company by the way :)(Duh totally forgot). Anyways this is what I'm facing to integrate. And if try to make databases talk with each other what problem can it cause?

Can you give me any comments?

A1: As a project manager you should always avoid thinking in terms of connecting back end servers, or whatever. This is this biggest single mistake that project managers make.

What you are actually doing is e.g. 'allow orders taken in Helsinki to be fulfilled in Brussels or St Johns Newfoundland depending on certain criteria about size and availability' i.e. a purely business objective. Only start talking about technical options when you have to. And then as little as possible.

In your case there is (we assume) some business driver that needs some connection between the processes served by your systems. You need to be very explicit about all the criteria before you move even an inch forward.

The answer to your question might be anything from send a few FTPs on a daily basis, to install SAP.

It certainly looks like you would get benefit from being able to connect some of the data. I must admit I thought CRM was supposed to do this. I think CRM is used nowadays to mean any old thing that lists customer contacts. So Option 1 is buy Siebel (a snip at 50 million).

The other approach I would look at is using a product that can take views across different databases. Given that all your databases are SQL I would think you could choose from loads of products. I might look first at Business Objects (I only assume it can run across databases/machines).

Actually merging the databases would not give you what you want which is some application than presents and manipulates the combined data. I suspect you will find that almost as easy to do with the separate databases as with one merged one.

A2: The fact that you have separate systems with different or the same technology and presumably on different servers is neither a good nor a bad thing. It is just the way your company has implemented its technical solutions to a set of business problems.

Before you talk about integrating databases (which may as edelwater suggests make it an EAI project) you need to define (or better have the business users with the check books define) a strong business reason for doing this.
Is there information in one or more database that you need to share with other databases?
Do people in different departments need access to a database they don't normally use?
Is there duplication of data between databases that is costing the business time and money to verify and control?
Are the separate databases costing the business money or damaging its reputation through operational errors?
Is there an operational cost in having separate databases that you could recover by combining servers or databases?

Do the separate databases create a disaster recovery and business continuity risk by not having a common checkpoint to roll back to and restore from if you have problems in your primary data centre?

I obviously don't know your business, but those are a few questions which might be sufficient to identify the business reason for making the systems talk to each other.

To treat this as a project management exercise you need to go through the following steps.
Identify the business drivers for the project.
Identify and approximately cost possible solutions.
Calculate if the benefits outweigh the costs and how long before the benefits can be realized.
If there is a mandatory business driver (e.g. legislation changes) or important strategic driver the project will probably go ahead even if it doesn't make money. Otherwise it is a business decision as to the best use of the company's money.

If you get through the steps above, you have a project and you can start talking about how you integrate data and databases and defining what data needs to be shared with which application.

A3: Here are a number of products and organizations that are good at bringing data together from disparate sources (Enterprise Application Integration). This normally involves an architectural layer of file based transfer or messaging between applications and databases. If you don't need close to real time interaction, you can build it for almost no external software expenditure using products like Perl or SQL Server's replication tools.

In my limited experience the process is never cheap as the analysis and design process is always very complex and you need to get the architectural design absolutely right. If you

are getting external integration experts in to help you, they
need to be given the business requirements and be taught
how the systems all work and how you use them before
they can make any significant progress. Remember that
you will be hiring them for their technical skills not for
their knowledge of your business.

Although many software vendors use relational databases,
they do not often do it to make the data more open to the
customer. They do it for performance, scalability,
portability and ease of upgrades. There is a reason they
deliberately obscure their database schemas. It is to stop
people looking inside the database and making changes
without using the front end application. Many (probably
most) application licenses are invalidated if you try to
reverse engineer or change the database without approval
from the software vendor.

Having said that, many application vendors provide export
and import utilities to transfer data in a safe way between
their system and external systems. Many vendors will also
give or sell you a fully documented database schema if you
speak to them and tell them why you want it. They are
keen to both protect the integrity of their product and keep
the customer happy and they can do that best by working
with you.

Note that if you are taking data from several databases, you
will almost certainly need to store it somewhere to allow it
to be merged together. I strongly doubt if any of the
application vendors would allow you to change their
databases. This means that you will need to design a new
database or make changes to your in-house service
provisioning system to hold the merging process.

After all that, I go back to the point I made a few days ago
and which I don't think you have addressed. You need a
very clear business requirement before you go much
further in this process. This integration will cost money

which should be spent in obtaining a business benefit o improvement of some kind. For example, one very simple question that needs to be resolved is how frequently the data is to be extracted from each database. A clear answer to that will resolve a number of basic architectural issues. Another question is whether you will rebuild your merged database every time or apply all the changes (inserts, updates and deletions) to it. The first option is simpler but more data intensive, the second option is more complex to design, build and test.

My suggestion is that unless you have a very strong set of business requirements; don't worry about integrating systems at the moment. The fact that you have a number of different systems with similar architectures is not a reason to merge them. In my house we have two cars and four bicycles. I would gain no benefit and enormous disadvantage from joining them all together. You may get the same effect from trying to join your systems together.

Question 79: Advice on Number of Staff to Hire

I'm in the planning phases of staffing-up for a small network support contract. The requirements are to deploy/maintain an integrated software development lab and provide end-user support.

My problem: I'm looking for industry data regarding how many support personnel it takes to support X many seats.

I estimate that there will be approximately 50 - 75 users in 3 locations (city-wide). The network will likely consist of a 4-5 site hub/spoke VPN configuration w/ T1s at each site.

Is this too much for 1 senior engineer and one junior engineer?

A1: It depends on your SLA (Service Level Agreements).

If you are talking about network activity it also depends on emergency status (1 hour) or standard 4-8 hour, next day etc. Are all 3 locations running the same systems?

If you support hardware, you must have at least 2 trucks (vans) stocked with appropriate repair/replace items and 2 Nextel radios wouldn't hurt. Do you repair items on-site or replace-repair or replace-send out?

You will be traveling between centers many times so be prepared with a "room" or office of your own at each.

For items that you cover but are not an expert in, find yourself a local on-call guru now.

If you have covered all these bases and more, I believe you can easily support your contract.

A2: If your network was properly planned you should be able to support this only with your senior engineer.

But I think you should look for outsourcing the service to any third party. A support contractor will have tools, personnel, vehicles, etc., and because of the fact that they are in the support business it is to expect they can do the job more efficiently.

Have you estimated how many thousand dollars per month is going to cost you one engineer with all associated cost (tools, training, spare parts, per-dime expenses, office space, etc.)? I'm sure you are going to be able to find the proper contractor for a lot less money.

About application development, this is a different business. Not too much technicians are good at LAN/WAN support AND software development. Maybe you should consider outsourcing this too, freelancers are very easy to find, and many of them make a very good job for a very convenient price. I've used freelance developers many times to provide my clients with complete solutions, and in general the experience was successful.

Question 80: PMP Braindumps

Does anyone know of a good PMP Braindump site?

A1: I've only heard of the term 'braindump' as a site where people report actual exam material. If this is what you mean, you may not be aware that the PMP professional code of conduct specifically prohibits this. If you contribute to a site such as this you would be stripped of your certification. I've heard of people for being reported for doing this even in one-on-one conversation.

A2: The primary value of any certification to the holder is to validate years of experience and knowledge in the workplace. From an employer's perspective, however, it is the perceived value of a given certification and what it brings to a particular company in helping meet the business objectives of that company, hence the financial component of the certification. Braindumps detract from this perceived value. Several well-known certificates have suffered due to the "braindump" mentality, the MCSE springing to mind immediately. The people who have labored, studied and strived for the right to the PMP certification are no more likely to participate in braindumping than they would participate in other illicit actions.

I believe that the vast majority of PMPs will not participate in braindumps because it is wrong, ultimately deteriorates the value of the certification and not because they are afraid of being stripped of their certification. That is a tool that PMI reserves to punish the transgressor, but realistically, the web is so fluid that most braindump sites will thrive anyway. Only if the people who have earned the right to wear the PMP lapel pin refuse to participate in this activity can it be stopped. Cisco certificates, at all levels, are among the most adamant about not participating in braindumps. A blatant request such as the one above will meet with instant flames on any Cisco certification group. These folks understand the value of a strong certification and protect it zealously.

As an adjunct instructor in the computer science department for a local community college, I tell my students to "Learn it and you will Earn it" in reference both to degree and certification tracks. To me, using braindumps to circumvent the requirements and true knowledge that only experience can bring is equivalent to cheating on exams. It is wrong and no one should support the lazy ones out there who are willing to cheat and are seeking PMP certification, or any other certification for that matter, merely for financial gain. So my advice for jflg and other braindumpers is to hit the books, be a project manager, meet the requirements to earn the PMP, and quit looking for the easy way out.

A3: On PMPCert, a Yahoo group, there is a freeware package called TranDumper. This program (along with a number of sample exams also available at the site) may be what you are referring to.

In any event ... when I was preparing to write the exam I tried a variety of different sources for tests and info on the exam.

Here's everything you need to know.

1. The new format has 200 questions (no change) with only a, b, c, or d answers (that's a change) and none of the answers is a combination such as "a and c".

2. If you have experience in working on projects (you have to document 4,000 hours if you have a degree) you will have learned just about everything you need to know ... except the theory. You will need to read a variety of materials for the theory -- but *most* (all?) of the theory is

mentioned (even if only in passing) in the PMBOK Guide.

3. I purchased a variety of materials and none of them was particularly useful. In fact, my experience was that a _full_ understanding of the PMBOK Guide (which you get when you join PMI) is sufficient to pass the exam.

In the end, I:

(a) memorized the 39 processes in the process groups and knew which were core and which weren't;

(b) took each chapter and highlighted and underlined all the detail information in each chapter;

(c) understood the flow from one core process to the next;

(d) understood the I,T&T,O well enough so that I could identify which outputs from one process became inputs to another process; and

(e) understood the EV equations.

A, C, D and E are simple memory work.

B requires reading and re-reading and re-reading each chapter in the PMBOK Guide. I spent about 2 hours reading the highlighted and underlined material in the PMBOK guide every day and writing out the 39 processes, equations, etc.

Looking back, I spent about 200 hours studying -- way more than I needed to pass, but just enough to make ne confident when I wrote the exam.

When I wrote the exam, the first two questions were like being hit by a baseball bat. The next 8 weren't much easier. After about 20 questions, the rest just seemed to fall into place and were easy to answer. At 2 hours 5 minutes, I had completed my first pass. I took a washroom break. I came back and did the ones I had left blank and revisited the ones I had tagged. By 2:25 I was done.

Question 81: Guesstimates vs. Estimates

Here's a typical scenario... I am called into a meeting, given a five minute (max) description of someone's concept for a new application. Then comes the inevitable question: How long will it take to write that?

I'm the only programmer in my organization. This is my first job out of college so I've never worked on a team before and all I know of how things are supposed to work is what I've read in books. Most of the time I'm being asked to do something I've never done before. I usually know it's possible but I need to research how.

As for my manager, he's one of the worst offenders. We've had many discussions on the subject. On the one hand, he tells me to just pad my estimates (which doesn't really help because I still have no idea what the real time frame is) and on the other hand, if I give him a number that he thinks is too high, he accuses me of being "difficult". He seems to think I should have learned how to give an accurate estimate in college.

The applications I'm being asked to design are mostly for in-house solutions to situations that arise. If I don't get them done on time, it only hurts my reputation. Occasionally, though, I'm asked to do something for an external client. Those are the worst, of course, because the job is usually bid based on my guess.

How do I get management to understand that without time to analyze the problem and determine the requirements, anything I say is nothing but a guess?

A1: Turn the situation back on them:

Ask "How many people (and which ones) will be assigned to work 100% on the project?"

Now you have them. When they tell you the people, your answer is that you want to discuss it with them because you need their input and until you have that you can't accurately predict how productive they will be.

Actually, it sounds to me as if you're being called into a marketing meeting. If that's true then the second method is to say that you and your boss have agreed that you will only prepare estimates -- verbal or written -- that he has asked you to do. (Naturally, you *do* discuss this approach well in advance with your manager. A good manager will protect his people.)

The third is to say, "Well, I'm up to my eyeballs on other work so I won't be working on it and since they'll be doing the work then you really should ask them."

In the red corner: Rock.
In the blue corner: Hard Place.

In the middle: You.

You're in a lose-lose situation. You can't say "All the text books and the stuff I've looked at on the internet say that any estimate at this stage is +/- 50%." Fact is: the text books and the internet do say that.

You can't say "This is my first job out of college and I'm still learning." Fact is: it is.

The best you can do, I think, is to give an estimate and add "But when I get further into the project, I will revise it and give you a more accurate estimate."

You could try developing your own algorithm. I did one for a language you've never heard of that basically took the number of files (one day each), number of transaction types (one day each) and number of reports (1 day each). There were a few other factors which had days or hours assigned to them. Then I validated it against work I'd already done and made some modes to my algorithm.

You could use a similar approach. Start with 1 day per screen, 1 day per table, 1 day for help screens, 1 day per report (it *always* takes a day to get a report to line up correctly) and see how accurately it works on projects you've already done and then modify it as appropriate. Remember: this is not just coding time we're estimating; this is coding, testing, compiling, debugging.

Remember to add time for end user documentation, your own department documentation, time for developing the distribution/installation file(s).

As a rule of thumb: for every 8 hours you are at work, you are productive for 5-6 of them. The rest get lost in downtime, administrative, shop talk, meetings, coffee runs. So, when you get the number of days, those are "100% dedicated" and you are not 100% dedicated.

You could also add "Let's allow two days for your department staff to do end user acceptance and a day for me to fix any bugs that they might find. If you want anything changed, that will increase the estimate. This looks like a really interesting project ... shall I get started on it now?"

A2: I am a meteorologist (via the Air National Guard) and a Project Manager (via my civilian career). First, the science of meteorology is well known and easily solvable by computer - 7 partial differential equations in 7 unknowns, HOWEVER, there is not enough input data to make accurate forecasts. 7-10 days out is about the best we're going to be able to do as far as weather forecasting, and being wrong could simply be the result of one or more very significant weather events slipping through our observation network.

Now, to the more difficult science of predicting project completion. First, any good project manager will add 20% slack to an estimate, and I agree with Peter Buetenhek as far as going into doubling if necessary. I realize that you may have established a standard by providing estimates on short notice, but perhaps you need to step back and ask them to let you consider the project and get back to them later that day. Unfortunately, saying something like "my first guestimate is 3 days" will result in your being held to 3 days even if later that day you increased the duration to 5 days. Remember to mark at least 2 days each month as non-working days, either because of sickness, personal appointments, company obligations, inclement weather, etc. In addition to scheduled holidays and vacation. In addition to the estimate. Further, the last week of the year rates ZERO productivity. Anything that gets accomplished then is a "gift".

You really need to stop giving the estimates in the meeting and prepare a brief "Concept" or "Charter" or "Scope" document before making an estimate. In fact, you can use that as your excuse the next time you miss a deadline and then respectfully request that you be given time to complete the "Concept/Charter/Scope" document in order to obtain agreement from the "Idea Man" that this is what is being requested before actually giving your estimate. It also gives you time to look for hidden glitches or other difficulties.

A3: Guestimating is an inexact science and those face to face on the spot meetings are always difficult to deal with.

You can make it better for yourself in the future if you keep a record of how much time (both elapsed days and actual effort) you put into your projects. Then in several months when you are asked, you can turn around and say "This sounds quite like project ABC which took <n> days". The more you measure, the better you will be able to tighten up your estimating process and make it much more repeatable which is what we are all aiming for.

Secondly, if you suspect that the manager or business user is not giving you the full details on the project up front (and they almost never do), get them to document their requirements. It is great how sitting down and writing can really make a person see the bigger picture and the little hurdles at the same time. You can make life easier for everybody by providing them with a document template and ask them to fill it in.

A4: Here's something I've used very successfully lately. It is a combination of things that have already been said. Start by finding out who will be the user of whatever you are programming.

Talk to that person (however briefly) about what they want, when they want it, and what it should do. Write it up as best you can.

Sit down with any good spreadsheet package and in one column put the name of each subset of code or function you will be creating.

In the column after it, put your best guess as to how long it will take.

In the next column put the word "Low", "Medium", "High"

to indicate whether that piece in your opinion will be easy, moderate, or complex to do.

In the next column take your original estimate and...
If low, copy it to this column
If med, multiply your estimate by 1.5
If high, multiply your estimate by 2.

Assuming you are working on it full-time, you can just add up the time and see how long.

Don't forget to add time for acceptance testing. I'd start with about 50% of the total dev time.

The result will likely not be an "accurate" estimate. What you will have is a primitive form of metrics based estimate you can measure your performance against. When the project is done, see how well the prediction matched up with reality. Wherever you were off, adjust the model accordingly. Keep using the same adjusted factors until you are seeing some correlation between estimate and reality.

I actually have done this a couple of times with good results over time. Accurate estimating is a process based on metrics tracked over time. It takes discipline and attention to detail most organizations just don't have.

Question 82: Using Project with Visio

I have a full project plan in MS Project right now. I am tracking 4 different parts of the project, which all have their own detailed tasks assigned. I need to be able to take all these tasks, and display them somewhere (I was thinking Visio) by their due dates. Originally, I just created my own Visio drawing and put each task in a box, and manually did it myself. This was ok - but the due dates are changing constantly, and that means I was manually changing my Visio drawing all the time which was very time consuming. I was wondering if there is a way to update my data in MS Project, and then export it and manipulate how I want it to display in Visio. Their timeline drawings don't work, because I need to see each task's detail just on the day it's due. OR- can Project do this all by itself? Can anyone help? I could even show you my original Visio drawing you you could see what I'm talking about.

The project is tracking 4 different pieces: Clinical, Financial, Interfaces, and Training. Each of these major pieces has each of their own detailed tasks assigned, which have due dates that change. For the calendar I want them in, each month is divided into 4 or 5 weeks - not by the day. I want those tasks (from all 4 pieces) to display in the correct due date it is assigned to, in either week 1 - 5, on my calendar. The fields I want to see in the task is the task number, the description and dependencies.

Can you help me?

A: P2002

File | Save As ...

Save as type: chose Excel Workbook and click on the Save button. This will start the export Wizard.

Click Next.

Click "Selected Data" (default); click Next.

Click "Use Existing Map"; click Next.

Click "Task 'Export Table' map"; click Finish.

As for the week number, choose one of the number fields. RightMouseButton on the column name and click on "Customize Field". This will bring up a popup window. Click on the formula button which will open up a window. Program your formula into it.

You'll have to modify the map to include the field (but that's no big deal now that you're this far along).

There's more data there than you actually need. You can edit Maps and create variations on them.

Question 83: Intranet Project Management

I'm curious about companies that use intranet sites to help manage Projects. I'd like to set one up for our engineering group.

Who maintains the page content?
How much time is involved on a monthly basis?
Can this be done as a collateral duty, or should someone be dedicated to the intranet?
What types of feedback have you gotten after implementing an intranet?

A: In our company we use Intranet and Extranet sites to manage projects.

We've got a Web Application called CDS (Software Development Control) whose purpose is to keep tracking of every single task of the project and time spent on every task. All engineers must do their tracking every day.

As we are a software development company, we ourselves give maintenance to site. But the content almost never changes. Sometimes we make improvements to the database architecture and to the business logic.

Once the intranet is build, most probably you won't need someone working on it every single day. I would dare to say that you just need someone to whom you can attend to when problems come out, if any.

Our Intranet application provides us with lots of information about costs, time and what people is doing every single day in any phase of the project.

The most difficult part is how do I use all this information?

How do I interpret all this data? How do I predict how a project is going to behave with this? What can I learn from this data?

Apart from CDS we also use another Intranet Application called Infoshare. It is a documental Intranet for the CMM and ISO procedures and templates documentation.

It's very helpful because all the company's procedures and document templates are always available for every single person in the company.

Before doing any of the steps recommended above (and they are all very good recommendations) you need to look at your internal processes.

If things are complex now, bringing in a software package will only add an additional layer of complexity. The software packages bring the ability to manage large volumes of data; they do not bring order out of chaos.

Step 1: What do you want to control and what steps can you take to do that in your existing environment?

Step 2: Do you have sufficient volume of information to justify a software package to manage the information volume?

Step 3: If you do bring in a package then it should be under the control of the PMO group. Support (backup, restore, rollouts, database recovery, etc.) is the responsibility of the IT group. End user use (data entry, extraction, reporting) is the responsibility of the PMO. Enhancements can (probably should) be handled as any other internal IT project.

Question 84: IT Methodology

I work in a hospital and we do no development work - everything we install is an existing commercial product. In the 6 years that I've worked here (lots more years in IT and as a PM before that) we've looked at and tried to use 4 or 5 different methodologies. None have been successful for one reason or another.

I'm facing a major system install later this year and am trying to come up with a proposal to try something different - hopefully something that works and am interested in seeing what others have used successfully for their IT projects.

Does anyone have, or have a reference to, a working project management methodology for IT projects?

A1: In some respects differing project management methods have their good and bad points. Some are weighted more to process rather than the production of actual artifacts. Some more aligned to quality and away from project financials. In my experience I have tried to take the best out of each methodology (RUP/ Prince2 / et other less known) and apply it to the circumstances that I am in at the time. However, I start with a one mission statement, ie a project is to deliver to the customer within cost, timescale and the customers quality expectations."

This may not answer your question, but hopefully will a shed some light upon the depth and breadth of project and program management and their retrospective relationship to IT as a whole.

A2: One word of caution, don't rely on methodology alone. There is not a 'best' methodology, but you should rather adapt it to your particular situation. If you tried several and none worked, you might have a more fundamental problem that is really understanding what the project you're managing is all about.

What problems specifically have you faced in past projects? Was scope creep a problem? Customer satisfaction? Cost overruns? Things like that can be minimized but not solved with a methodology. If you could be more specific as to what you want to accomplish in this project we can give you better advice.

A3: IMO the methodology you want to/have to use depends on the type of project. Some types of applications dictate a specific type of process. The existing models doesn't give you the exact recipe for your project, it's just a general method proven to be working for certain types of projects.

In my PM classes we had a look at Pressman's classic "Software Engineering - A Practitioner's Approach" which describes many different methodologies and even gives you an example of which one is good for what.

You should do a post-mortem of your projects (usually time gives you a better perspective) to see what went wrong so you can pinpoint a specific problem. You cannot reject a methodology just because it didn't work on a certain project.

Question 85: Team Building exercises for tense situations

I am managing a team of several technical people on a technical software development project. This is a new project, only a few weeks into it, and there are already personality conflicts developing.

I'd like suggestions for some team building exercises that we can do in our team meetings that only take 15 minutes or so, but are fun, get to know each other types of exercises that help relieve the tension so we can get back to dealing with the project.

Any Suggestions?

A1: I would start by looking at the issue from a different angle. That is, whether you have the right project structure and resource base.

Are the people being "difficult" because they are under-utilized or overworked? If people do not have clear and achievable challenges they will get bored or frustrated and most will not be able to articulate the cause of their problems.

Are there bottlenecks in the project structure that are causing some people to experience frustration by making it difficult to accomplish tasks or creating delays? And are the standard processes and structures on the project well defined and clearly explained to everyone? If, for example, your quality process requires a code review but the coding standards are not well written and understood or if the process focuses on the individual who has written the code rather than the code itself, there is a clear opportunity to improve things and get the personalities focused on the job. I am not saying there is a problem with your quality process, this is just an example.

Have you done a skills analysis (it doesn't have to be formal and overly structured) to ensure that your team have the skills to do the jobs required of them and that they are not working at too high or too low a level for their abilities? In these tough times there are some very experienced people doing jobs at a much lower level than they have done for a long time. This can cause problems if they think they are still senior decision makers.

Are inexperienced team members getting appropriate mentoring and guidance to help them pick up speed?

Is your architecture and overall design documented and accepted by the project team? It can be very negative to have a person on the project not knowing why they are doing a task or convinced that they are building something that will not work properly.

Is your project schedule aggressive but achievable? Nobody is going to do their best work if told they have to run 1500m in two minutes. Likewise, if told to run 1500m in 15 minutes, they won't try hard enough.

Are you in control of all the processes and resources on the project? If you have a dependency on an external group or person, this can cause a lot of problems if they don't deliver on time or to the defined level of quality.

I am not downplaying team building. I think it is an essential part of running a successful project and in my experience, a team that bonds well will produce excellent results.

There are plenty of things you can do with a team that don't necessarily involve taking the team to the pub and getting them drunk. You can have occasional meetings at a local coffee shop; have a cooking competition (a different person has to bring some home made product to the team meeting each week); institute a series of fines and rewards for trivial and fun activities (for example anyone wearing a blue shirt on Wednesdays has to pay a forfeit).

There are lots of things that you can do like that to get people having fun together, but the first place that I would be looking is at the structure of the project.

A2: One of the best team exercises i can remember was to get each person to write 3 things about themselves that none of the team would know.
This is usually done on flip charts.
Once the team returns they all have to guess who the team member is by looking at the evidence.
It's possible to find out quite a lot about people in this exercise.

Don't worry too much about ego's etc its path of the course in project situations. Everyone should be equal in a project situation but that rarely happens it success of the project is more important than bruised ego's.

A3: While those posed "situation" exercises are sometimes helpful, I've always HATED their artificiality and contrived qualities, AND I find their usefulness limited by those qualities.

I like the answer that talked about skills evaluation, but that is less help immediately. The answer I often get back to is the rule of thumb, 'the team that can laugh together can work together'. The best team-building exercises that I've ever found were simple, like monthly office potlucks, or monthly lunch-outs. If someone is just in a bad mood that day, they can bow out, but the door is still open next time. The key is allowing democratic choice (that's why the potluck). Also key is relaxed, non-work face time.

Team-building exercises are valuable in emergency situations, but should be run by a professional, not internally. If you run it and it doesn't work, things may get much worse.

Question 86: Development Proposal

Does anyone have any good recommendations where to start to start writing up proposals? I guess maybe I am looking for a template, somewhere to start as I have just started looking for outside contract work and unbeknownst to me, the feedback was / is amazing.
Can anyone help me starting out in the wonderful world of documentation?

A1: I follow a fairly standard approach:

Letter explaining following proposal:
- Thanks for opportunity;
- Listening to your concerns I can see x, y, and z is critical in this project
- The proposal is broken into the following sections;
   1) Intro (state the problem/challenge);
   2) Proposed solution (overview);
   3) Scope of work (more detailed);
   4) Assumptions (critical elements that define what client is responsible for/what you are responsible for);
   5) Schedule & Fees
     a) How change orders are handled;
     b) Payment schedule
   6) Authorization
     a) client signature/date with clause

Client agrees to pay contractor/company x based on the payment schedule in section 5. Final payment is due x days after completion of Section 3 scope of work (or immediately upon completion);

A note about proposals. Gauge the size of the project before taking extensive time to give a proposal. For small projects (you determine), do not create multiple page proposals. A simple 1 page letter estimate is adequate.

You don't want to spend 2 days creating a proposal for even 1 week of work. I use a rule. If the project is less than 1 month in duration, I give a 1 page letter with authorization.

A2: I am working with Grey Matter India Technologies Pvt. Ltd as Strategy Head. Proposal is a very sensitive document and it has to very informative and sales oriented. The following sessions are part of any standard proposals.

A. Introduction
------- Introduction to both your firm and client firm

B. Scope of the document
------- Briefly explain scope of the document

C Overview
------- Give an outline of proposal

D Understand
--------- Define your understanding about client requirements. These are based on certain assumptions and RFP you have received from your client.

E Business Analysis
-------- Your analysis of client existing business process and business model

F Industry Analysis
-------- Depth Industry analysis to prove your industry knowledge

G -Enterprise Requirements

--- Elaboration of client requirements
H - Business Strategy

Technical Strategy
Technical Feasibility
Existing Infrastructure
Technology Risk

I- Proposed Solution
   Overview
   High Level Architecture
   Tools and Technology
   Design Methodology
   Project Management
   Project Organization Structure
   Deliverable Matrix

J- Commercials
   Estimation Methodology
   High Level Estimation
   Communication Plan
   Terms and Conditions
        From Client Side
        From GMI
K -Credentials
L -Annexure

Question 87: Non-IT trained in IT Project Management

I am a UK-chartered quantity surveyor & builder based in Singapore. Some 3 years back, I joined a government body's IT development department. My role was to kick-start its e-business program, to raise IT & e-business adoption in the industry. My functions were a mix of program management, product marketing and management, promotion and event management.

However, plans are aloof to merge my department with the Information Systems Department (which is really the 'techie' unit). Recently, I'm tasked with manage system development projects complete with programmers, system analysts, system users and external stakeholders. And I'm not talking small projects but valued at US$1000,000-300,000 range. There are 3 and even include a mobile solution development.

I am afraid that a lack of IT qualification will not just hinder my chance of promotion but also put me at risk at being booted out. I hold a MBA (double specialization in e-business and techno-entrepreneurship) but this is more focused on business issues. I've managed vendors before but it's more on the client side and less formal and more hands-off.

I do not relish the thought of going back for an IT degree. Which options are available to me? Would a PMP (PMI) or IT Project+ (CompTIA) help? Which would be better, which should I target first?

Do I really need to get an IT degree or at least a Diploma in, say, System Analysis?

A1: I would say, if you are a truly skilled PM, the techie degree won't be of much value to you. While understanding some specific technology issues, especially around application development would be of benefit. If you want to do the "Crash course", I'd recommend taking a week, and doing a MS Certification type course, or at least MS training in the tool suite you expect your developers to use. Not for the purpose of becoming a developer, or telling them how best to do it, but to understand what it is they do, and how they go about it.

I have always maintained that an excellent PM does not need specific skills in the area that they are working in. (i.e. a truly talented PM could just as effectively lead a project to develop a 20 story building as they could lead a $20million dollar IT development.) You are no more the carpenter, than you are the application developer. Stick to what you know, and concentrate on that. Any IT skills you can acquire will certainly help you along the way, but I have known, and worked with some extremely talented PMs in my day that were not "Technical" at all, yet have been extremely successful leading technology development project in excess of $3million dollars. So, don't sweat it.

Focus on what you know. Draw from that knowledge base. Use your leadership abilities. You'll do fine.

A2: There is no need to get a formal qualification just because the remit is changing slightly.

Stick to the "what you know" side of the job, the processes and procedures and you will quickly find that these will fit in to all type of work, whether it's IT or Marketing etc...

As you start to work with new technologies you will find yourself picking up real life experiences and these are worth far more these days that the qualification pieces of paper.

A3: There are two roads I think you should go down. First, I'd do the PMP certification. Then, I'd do some application specific course, like Microsoft .NET, or C# development, something to get you to understand what developers do in their daily lives. Understanding what they do will go a tremendous length in your ability to gauge the amount of time tasks take, and what the daily life of the "Programmer" is all about. It just makes managing projects easier. Once you understand development, and what the life cycle of development is all about, you'll have no problems.

I've been a developer for over 15 years, and a PM for over 10, as well as a senior leader (CIO) in my organization now for over 7. I can appreciate the position you are in. You will do fine.

A4: Please allow me to suggest a few thoughts and questions to ask yourself.

How do you really feel about the risk of being merged with the other group? From my experience, your statements about not having the IT background may be symptomatic of a greater obstacle.

If you understand the project management side well, do you think those skills would be greatly impacted by the "venue" change? Asked differently, when we PMs start work on a project, is it better to define scope, cost, and schedule on our own or with the reliance on experts of the focus area (in this case IT techies)?

Although certifications are an appropriate approach to obtaining a great quantity of information quickly, what risk are you willing to bear for the event of when the book-smarts comes up against the reality of street-smarts built responsiveness, which often provides more effectiveness?

Finally, consider the level of personal risk you may be worried about. My career approach has been one to rely on what I know first and then expand from that to new areas. Two decades ago, my mentors showed me to understand work is work and not much more. They forced me to look at challenges like you described as having only one real potential obstacle, failure. As I learned, if I could accept failure as a learning process instead of a personal reflection, I would greatly improve my chances of surviving the changes. Reflecting on my experience, this approach has served me well.

A5: I don't believe that technical skills are vital for an IT project manager.

The most important thing is that you appreciate the work being done for you by your IT staff. If I've been told once, I've been told 100 times, that "it's not rocket science". My response to that is that its closer to rocket science than you think.

Respect your staff, their skills, and their commitment, and they will respect you and do their best.

I would rather work for someone with no technical skills who was a good listener, than for a Bill Gates "wannabee" who doesn't respect me.

I also don't think a 'crash course' is necessarily helpful. A little knowledge is truly a dangerous thing, especially in the hands of someone who doesn't know that they only have a little knowledge.

I once had a lawyer (I work in the IT dept of a law firm) try telling me what database structure to use. He had dabbled in VB and thought he knew enough to tell me how to design the tables. He got every detail incorrect - he thought it should be done in VB - not MS Access!

They say 'Love conquers all'. In the workplace I say 'Respect Conquers All'.

A6: In studying for the PMP certification, you will learn very little about IT, in and of itself.

Your IT colleagues may be, for a time, impressed with your PMP credential, in and of itself, until the patina wears off, and it's clear to them that they're teaching you everything they know, even though on paper you look better than them.

As noted above, they will for perpetuity be impressed with your organizational and people skills if you apply them in a manner that makes their jobs/lives easier, and enables them to focus more on the wizardry that turns them on, as opposed to what they perceive as the "administrative drivel" that you and I both know frames the essence of a successful project.

Your IT colleagues will help you learn, if you demonstrate curiosity and respect.

There is no way you can catch up to them in their specialties, though you could learn about how the technology in their specialties has evolved to lead to today's state of the art, as well as where it's headed in the short-term; this will pay dividends by positioning you to be able to see things as they see them, and more effectively "walk that mile in their moccasins" that so often leads to effective leadership and decision.

After you master the basics, you might consider an emerging technical specialty to master for yourself. It should be one that's just getting off the ground. For example, I know tons of non-technical people that had never used a computer until they started to be mass-marketed. Within a couple years, a number of these people became html gurus, because it was so new, and so few people were experts at the time.

Again, in line with what's been said above, don't try to do this with a motivation of beating them at their game, or prove yourself superior, but strike that happy medium of coexistence and mutual respect.

Question 88:   The benefit of PMP certificate

I am curious about the PMP certification. I do project management in my current position for a very small company, and think it might be a nice certification to possess. (When I'm out of school for too long, I start to get bored.)

What is everyone's opinion on this? Why are you working through the process? A job requirement? Better pay? Prestige?

A1: I have been on the certification trail for years, albeit in more technical pursuits, and have earned numerous certifications. However, I pursued the PMP certification because I felt it was a validation of years of experience and self-study in the PM arena and because my CIO told me in a performance appraisal that she wanted me to become more knowledgeable in formal PM practices. After some research, I determined that the PMP was the certification that would accomplish both of these goals. I started working on the cert in early 2001 and finally took the test last December. Although many IT shops don't deploy formal PM, particularly in the WAN/LAN space, my company has started to projective all of our divisions and it was a natural fit to mold our IT PM methodology along the PMBOK lines. I feel that the lessons I learned along the PMP certification path helped me immediately as I applied them to my current projects and they will continue to help me in the future.

Passing the test on the first try was obviously a relief, but the journey to the exam is what made the experience worthwhile. Was it worth the effort, for me the answer is yes, definitely, but only you can answer that for yourself. It sounds like you are committed to life-long learning, just as

I am, and that is always a good thing for your career. Regardless of whether you choose to earn the PMP or not, remember certificates come and go, but true knowledge lasts forever.... you just have to keep updating it

A2: Like most things in life, a PMP does not guarantee much of anything. It does provide some input to a prospective employer, customer, or colleague that you have met some professional standard within project management. It also provides you with a common language other PMPs use to communicate with. In my case, it was a tangible affirmation that I am serious about promoting and practicing a professional brand of project management. Hopefully, in the future, it will provide me with a way to differentiate myself from other job applicants but that, to me, is a secondary consideration.

Project management is one of those areas in the workplace crying out for some order and standards. As you may know, quite a large percentage of projects fail. In the long run, this only tends to discredit the role of project manager. Especially with senior management has presided over many of these failed projects.

So those of us who are serious about doing this job right, ought to subscribe and promote professional standards by any means we can.

Question 89: Outsource or in-house development

My IT team is in a dilemma now...we have a large web application that we want to develop within the next 6 months. Our initial plan was to outsource to a web development company. But it turns out, even the best company out there is disappointing...they are dishonest and not as proficient (skills-wise) as we hoped.

Now we're considering developing it in-house. We have 2 relatively inexperienced programmers (I'm one of them) but no project management experience.

Would it be suicide to try to develop something like this in-house by managing it ourselves and hiring part-time programmers to help out?

We plan to send ourselves for project management and applications architecture courses, but is knowledge sufficient to overcome inexperience?

A1: Project success is highly dependent on the project manager understanding the details of the work to be done, and, to a large degree, having strong technical skills in both the focus area, as well as the sub-disciplines that also touch the project. Without the former, one cannot effectively plan the project (well, that's a little extreme; you could use "spiral development"--plan the project based on what you know now, then multiply the budget and timeline by three to accommodate the changes you'll need to make while you "learn as you go", and continually update budget/timeline). Without the latter, one cannot successfully manage the project team.

Based on the internal environment you describe, this project should be contracted.

If, by saying "...out there..." you mean the local environment, then you need to relax your selection criteria to include contractors from outside the area, and expect to pay travel costs, etc. accordingly. There are many strong development firms of all sizes; attracting the good ones to work on your project, without paying through the nose for the privilege of their association, is the challenge!

Have you considered doing an RFI, to see who's out there in the marketplace, or thought of Dunn & Bradstreet listings, etc. as a means to identify possible contractors? There are a variety of web-available RFI, RFP, RFQ, etc. templates; other departments in your company may have some boilerplate, too.

A2: My early project management experiences were very inefficient, and frustrating to some degree, because I hadn't yet been exposed to any of the formal techniques one can apply to ease project planning, scheduling, resource commitment, execution, and verification efforts.

Thus, I went with my intuition, and found myself doing many of the critical steps using common sense and gut feel as my guide (though I didn't realize I was until later on when I got some formal training). However, I ended up iterating a lot, applying trial and error over and over until I developed a task planning/tracking template that worked, and in general working a lot harder than I needed to, given the projects' relative complexities.

Enough said about my history, but a little more about my background--I'm a PMP, and a Registered Professional Engineer.

In my professional opinion, you need a consultant to help you organize this project's scope and procurement. Either that, or your company needs to hire someone versed in project management, especially if the new system is to be one of your organization's "flagship" applications.

Some observations that back up this bold statement:

You may be experiencing "scope creep" instead of technical limitations on the part of your contractor. Have you ever written down and formally signed any statement of work? Until this gets nailed down in black and white, you'll continue to be challenged by explaining things "over and over" to the contractors.

You may also be experiencing "scope creep" and contractor ineffectiveness due to a lack of internal consensus on what is supposed to be done. In a situation where the deliverables aren't formally documented, the contractors in essence have multiple customers, and multiple potentially asynchronous deliverables lists, one for every person in your company they come in contact with. What you're experiencing could be a result of the contractors continually jumping from one brush fire to the next, with limited overall direction.
-Are the contractors working on a time and materials basis, or for an hourly/weekly rate? If so, you're doubly challenged because they have no incentive to ever bring the project home.

Just curious, but why the recurrent theme on "first time project management experiences" in both your initial and reply posts? No offense, but to some degree I'm left wondering if I'm helping a colleague with a real-world problem, or providing fodder for a project management course developer.

A3: Project management skills are learned through personal experience, mentors, courses and training, native intelligence/common sense, and trial & error.

You haven't mentioned budget considerations. Is there enough money available to hire an adjunct resource to work alongside you, to temporarily augment the team with project management skills for just this project? You could "mentor" with this person, lay the groundwork for a standard project management approach for the future, and get the app development done at the same time.

Sounds like a great opportunity for you to shine, by both providing wisdom about how to organize the effort, and also implement the foundations of standard project management practices within your company's business processes for the future. Sounds like you also have a great opportunity to learn by doing, and expand your skill set.

If no money is available to hire a mentor to work beside you, learn as much as you can as quickly as you can about project management. Surely there must be someone there that has managed a project before? Find them, get them to show you how they did it previously (tools, techniques, document templates, etc.), expand on what they did based on what you think could be done better, and start the project.

A4: As a "techie" with 20 years experience in networking and programming, I find that using consultants is a total waste of time and money. When I contracted out a Frame Relay project, my RFC made specific statements about what was to be done. I didn't want to get phone calls at 3AM reporting a router is down and run into the office to fix it...but in the end, after 5 months of fighting over contract terminology I flew all over the country setting up the routers and configuring the networks myself.

When I began a web project I contracted out to a company that had the skills and all the right endorsements and recommendations...but when they got the project, they finally admitted they were doubtful my project was possible. I was amazed because it was a simple web site that remembered your profile and purchase history. I took it back and completed the project in 4 months.

So my advice, based on a multitude of over-priced, inflated ego's and under qualified consulting firms...learn the skills, take those classes, and jump on board. Make sure your management team knows this is a new challenge for you and that it won't run as smooth as glass...but the more you do this, the more you learn, the better you get. When you reach that point where you are well rounded and very versed in many aspects of IT, you are one valuable guy!

Organizing your time and others is easy. Hire a few part timers (well qualified and experienced temps) and have them work in your office so you can watch their progress. That's the solution I came up with many years ago and it has worked wonderfully.

A5: I've done it both ways. I managed one of the first successful web projects for my type of governmental organization four years ago, got national recognition and my team got all kinds of (small) bonuses. I've also been both a buyer and seller of contractor services and have +30 years as a tech, and a manager. All of that counts, and I find I have to use every trick and technique I ever learned to pull off outsourced projects.

Outsourced development does not save you money. It may save development time. But in order to realize any advantage you need to have your technical and business requirements nailed, and you need to know how to do contract negotiation/administration. If you don't have that down cold, you will either fail, or get eaten up in the change request process. When you go outside, you lose the ability to fix requirements/design mistakes on the fly. A smart vendor will be very willing to add functionality, for a price. And I've seen a lot of projects fail right there. Scope creep is bad for starts, it's murder when the meter's running.

My advice is to start small, and build expertise. Plan to throw the first one away. You've probably heard that before, but somehow people refuse to believe it.

Question 90: Resource allocation

I am looking from a hint from anybody as to how I may do this.
I am looking to have a master and subprojects project where each person in the team will create their own project (sub) and the overall team will be the Master. I am looking to calculate for each member in the master how much of their time has be allocated so I manager of the Dept make look up and allocate the next project to the person with the lowest % allocated.

Can you help?

A: From what you have said it looks like you need a resource pool. I have managed something similar whereby I have 9 projects being managed in my team and would like to see where my resources are allocated and how much time they are working on these projects.

Basically create a blank project plan with no information in it. Save it as 'Team Resource Pool.mpp' for instance. Keeping your 'Team Resource Pool' open go into each of you team members perspective project plans and go to 'Tools' then 'Resources' and click on 'Share Resources'. A new dialog box will appear called 'Share Resources' click the tick box next to 'Use Resources' and then select the 'Team Resource Pool.mpp' from the 'From' list.

This will now list all of your resources and their tasks for that project on the 'Team Resource Pool.mpp'. To view these open the 'Team Resource Pool.mpp' project plan and select the 'Resource Usage View' to successfully view all resources and their project allocations.

Continue this process on all your project plans you wish to report to you 'Team Resource Pool'.

Question 91: Novice Project Planner

I have just been pushed into designing and implementing a project plan. Where do I start?

I was going to take some courses or pick up a book, but I don't have that kind of time. I need to learn about project planning and deployment in a few hours.

Any suggestions on documentation which I can download and read it?

A1: Here's a template for writing up a project proposal; it will also work as a means to write up a project statement:
Project Name = ?
Project Statement = In one sentence each, explain what is to be done, what the project's goals are, and what the minimum deliverables must be in order to consider the project successful.
Current Situation = How are things now?
Scope of Work = What do you plan to do to change the Current Situation? What will the project's end product be?
Estimated Costs = How much do you think the project will cost, and why?
Benefits and Risks = What do you hope to gain by doing the project, what could go wrong, and how will you address the contingencies if they occur?
Initial Project Plan, Roles and Responsibilities = Who is expected to do what, when, and for how long?

Scheduling a project isn't much different from organizing your "Things To Do" list for your days off. Sit quietly for an hour, and jot down anything/everything you can think of that needs to be done, then sequence the list so it can be done as efficiently as possible and so it reflects "dependencies" (things that must happen before/after other tasks). Next, estimate how long it will take to do each thing, pick a start date, and then estimate the project schedule based on the task sequence and task durations you estimated.

A low-end, though effective, tool for doing this on relatively small, linear projects is MS Excel. I type my thoughts in, put sequential numbers in next to the steps, sort all the data and write the sequence numbers until I'm happy they're in the right order, and then estimate the durations.

If you understand the work pretty well, then duration estimating will be your bigger challenge. I usually do a "best guess", then augment that with an optimistic (if everything went really, really fantastic, how fast could I get it done?) and a pessimistic (if everything goes really, really bad, what's the worst-case longest time I think this task could take?) estimate. Then combine the duration estimates as follows to compute the task duration to include in your plan:
Plan Task Duration = [Optimistic Duration + (4 * Best Guess Duration) + Pessimistic Duration]/6

This, too, can be coded in Excel.

One may be tempted to use the Pessimistic estimates for everything, but that's inappropriate because it's not fair to the customer. My approach is an accepted standard practice that accounts for uncertainty in the estimates, and thus protects both the estimator/project manager and the customer.

A2: In your case, I would buy the step by step guide to ms project.

In it simplest manner using MS project:

Break the tasks downs into phases.
Then break the phases down into tasks.
When setting the durations give a little lea way, but make it realistic, you may need to research
if people need to travel then take this as another task.

Look at your resources, they normally fall into the following categories:
people, equipment, materials, rooms.

Assign the people equipment material and rooms
Making sure you appreciate the difference between
effect driven 2 people working on a project the time halves.
Non effort driven, traveling from Manchester to London
does not reduce if more people are in the car.

If you do not have enough resources, or can not meet the time scale given, then pray. Be careful of responsibility without authority. Go back to your manager and state what resources or extra time you need. Do not give them problems only solutions.

This is a very simplified way to create a basic plan.

A3: To get you up and running with a plan. Look at the scope of the work to carry out within the plan. Draw yourself a work-break down structure. This WBS can be in phases and also include products. Then consider how this WBS reflects the organization of your teams. From this comparison you should be able to allocate responsibilities into the WBS. This allows you and the person responsible for delivering the plan to discuss and define the activities, timescales, logic, resources etc. Remember although you prepare the plan you may not be the owner.

A4: PMI considers the project plan to be the entire plan document, but many people who use automated tools such as MS Project use the phrase project plan to mean the MS Project Schedule. If you don't have much time, the best place to start is really the same place to start if you do: the Project Charter.

Many of the other sites mentioned in this and other posts show a Project Charter template. The point is to get an overview - 1 or 2 pages - to make sure all project stakeholders (steering committee, management, project manager, team members, customers) have the same understanding of the project at a high level. If you don't do this first, you will likely find yourself doing a lot of re-work, and taking all the blame for any misunderstandings.

The preferred method of creating a Project Charter is to sit down with the Project Sponsor/Steering Committee, ask open-ended questions, and hash out the wording during the meeting. But often you have to take a stab at it yourself and then meet with them to modify it. So the Project Charter helps you create a shared understanding of the project at the outset, then it remains your touch point throughout the project, as expectations invariably change during the project. Most of the remaining Project Plan documents flow from the Charter, such as the Scope document, the WBS, SOW, Roles & Responsibilities, Schedule, and Budget. When conflicts arise, you look to the Project Charter rather than get into individual opinions and finger-pointing.

Question 92: Logical relationships between tasks

Does anyone know if MS Project 2000 can support logical relationships between tasks?

For example, we have a project that involves 4 what-if tests. There are 4 possible ways to solve a problem. If anyone of these works, great. Then the other tests are un-necessary and we can continue on with the project. So not all tests start at the same time or have the same duration. So we have scheduled each test to begin as-soon-as-possible.

My schedule looks like this:

Preliminary work ->

AND

Test 1

OR

Test 2

OR

Test 3

OR

Test 4

AND

Final work ->

We won't know the results of test 1 until after tests 2 and 3 begin, but we can always cancel tests 2, 3, and 4 in mid-stream.

A1: I don't think you can do what you want in Project 2000 using basic functionality.

However, I have been working with VBA under Project 2000. It can be done with VBA but it will tend to be involved. You can set up a VBA macro that runs every time the project calculates. When the macro sees one of the tasks reach 100% completion, it can mark the rest of them as 100% or delete the others that you no longer need.

Another alternative might be to have all the tasks organized under a summary task. That should make them easier to manage as a group. Link the follow on tasks that occur after the tests to the summary task. When one of the tests works out ok, delete the others. The summary task should assume a completion of 100% and the follow on tasks should be affected accordingly.

A2: I found that by organizing the different options under a summary tasks, it was easier to manage. Since there were 4 different tests, I simply linked only one test to the follow on tasks. Then I would print out my Gantt chart. Then I would unlink that test and link the next test. Then print the next option Gantt chart. I did this for all 4 tests. Like I said, this worked pretty well. Once the tests were completed, the unsuccessful tests (tasks) were deleted from the project.

A3: I know this an older post but incase someone else runs into the problem. I use the Finish-Finish relation ship for this. I will mark the bar chart correctly, but does not fill in the dates on the task listing. I would right the project like this.

Predecessors

1 - work
2 - test one   1
3 - pass test one   2,6FF,9FF
4 - fail test one   2
5 - test two   1
6 - pass test two   5,3FF,9FF
7 - fail test two   5
8 - test three   1
9 - pass test three   8,3FF,6FF
10 - fail test three 8
11 - more work   2,5,9

But for every project manager there is a different way to do the same task.

Question 93: Need help on MS Project

I'm new on MS Project.
I have to roll-out 10 applications in 35 countries.
Some colleagues will go in countries to install applications.
I want to plan this activity in MS Project.
I want to avoid the installation of two different applications
in a country at the same time.
One person can't be at Boston and Paris in the same time.

What scenario of representation can you advise me?

A1: If I'm reading your question correctly, you are
unaware that MS Project is just a calculation and display
tool. You still need to do upfront planning and data entry
to identify all your resources, tasks, hours, and precedence
relationships.

1. To avoid scheduling the same person in Boston and Paris
at the same time, enter each installer as a separate resource.

2. You have to add a precedent task of travel time to each
install task if you want to allow for that.

3. To avoid installing 2 apps at once you can either assign
both to the same installer or link the install of one app as
the precedent of another.

A2: NEVER EVER try to go back in time with MS
Project after you have entered "Actual Work".

In other words, once you have your project laid out, you
might realize that someone did something a month ago
that was never in the project. Don't add it to the project as
a task that happened before the current date. I cannot

remember what the exact problem I had was, but it really made a mess of things. I usually add it to the bottom of the project, then assign it 0 hrs of work (a milestone), then add a note stating that it was completed by such-in-such on such-in-such day and it took n hrs.

Question 94: Iterative vs. Waterfall process models

For some time I have been debating and trying to understand these two process models, their similarities and differences and when and how to use them in the real world of managing software development projects.

I am of the opinion that academia has misrepresented and confused these models. Here is my take.

In projects where the problem space is understood and predictable (more or less :)) the Waterfall is appropriate.

In projects where the problem space is uncertain and unpredictable say in the case of new technology the Iterative model is usually used to identify and resolve problems that occur because they haven't been anticipated.

At the same time, in the Waterfall model we follow the steps until we run into a problem. When this happens the model requires that you go back to the beginning (Scope) and start all over, redefining the problem. You repeat this until you have no more problems and the project is complete. This sounds pretty iterative to me. SO...what is the difference...what am I missing?

From my chair, they all sound the same.

I am considering the use smaller project scopes and having several iterations. Each iteration contains additional features. Rather then having one huge deliverable of 110 features at the end of the year, I am breaking it up into iterations of about 20 features released at 3 month intervals. Is this then an iterative model...I would say not because it is independent of the problem space of the process model.

It seems to me that projects with that require longer then six months to complete have a higher probability of failing.

What's your insight?

A1: To me, "iteration" does NOT mean starting over with the problem statement. It means repeating certain steps-- at any point in the development lifecycle, but especially in the design phase--until, in Steve McConnell's phrase, "users get excited". So it means giving them a prototype, incorporating feedback, giving them another prototype, incorporating feedback, etc. until they are happy. You may iterate a key document, say a project charter, until everybody is happy.

Your example of breaking a project into phases where features 1-50 are delivered, then features 51-65, etc., is not iteration, IMHO. Taking those first features, working with the users through successively detailed designs IS iteration.

Also, you mentioned a 6-month project, the rule of thumb I've heard is try and deliver features at least every 6 weeks.

A2: Here's my historical perspective. I heard of "waterfall" in the 80's as what had been done in the 70's. Back then, there was not as much stress on programmers interacting with the end users. The reason is that the programmer was hip-deep in any existing system, and knew it as well as the users, and knew their workflow, etc. So a lot of times the programmer acted as the SME (subject matter expert) and had the time and freedom to design what he (or she, but mostly he!) felt was the next step in automation. "Iterative" simply meant that you would go back to an earlier phase when you hit a bug or decided to add functionality. Very few people are brilliant enough to conceive a perfect design, so some problems found in later stages would cause you to go back to that step and flow the new requirement forward through the steps you completed on the rest of the design. This was referred to as "iterative".

Decades later, most people building apps are hired guns, and the underlying technology is so much more advanced that they don't have to know the workflow or the data to get the job done. So it's much more important to work with the users, who are not necessarily skilled in expressing their requirements clearly and completely. So we have "prototyping", which is successive approximations of the entire app in a way the user can relate to, rather than just a conceptual design. Prototyping is planned as entirely iterative.

I didn't think that "true" waterfall ever existed, as it did not allow for iteration at all. I thought it was a model that explained that you have to analyze before designing, design before building, build before testing, etc. My understanding was iteration was what allowed the waterfall model to be fitted to reality.

On prototyping, you might analyze, design, code, test - show to client -
modify code, test -
show to client -
analyze additional requirements, design, modify code, test -
etc.

In prototyping, your cycles are so brief, days or weeks vs. months or years, that it hardly makes sense to designate separate stages. In mainframe app development, you could be in the design stage for months, doing nothing except design. In the coding stage, you could be coding for a year and nothing else. Remember, the original programs weren't strictly modular, so testing a subroutine was sometimes more work (stubbing out the code, creating dummy input) than it was worth. Going back to analysis or design was something you strove to avoid because of its time-consuming nature. Remember, we didn't have even the basic drawing or text-editing tools (Visio, MS Project, Word) that we have now either. You might actually have a secretary retyping a design document, and a systems analyst using a plastic template to re-draw the flow. Now the tools make it pretty simple to build something, throw it at the wall, and see what sticks, so that's how a lot of people actually work.

A3: The waterfall approach really does exist! Bear in mind that while most of us think in terms of IT projects, I think you will find it hard to iterate the process of building a road, bridge, etc. In other words, in the wider world of project management there is a broad spectrum of approaches ranging from one extreme to another. I would say that the PM must get to know the customer, the contract, the project P&L, and the team well enough to choose the best approach for all parties. There is no question in my mind that choosing an approach, gaining client and team approval, and sticking to it throughout the project is a great way to avoid the kind of craziness that leads to a lot of heartache.

I personally don't believe any one approach is "better" than another. I have worked on projects that were 3 months long and more than 2 years long. The only thing that matters from the PM point of view is to listen to your team, the client, and the other stakeholders. In the end, getting the job done and striking the kind of balance that satisfies the client, makes money, and delivers results is the only way to prevail. It certainly isn't easy but, hey, that's what a PM is for.

A4: Take a look at the Rational Unified Process which among others considers iterative development to be a "best practice" (and I fully agree).

Iterative development means dividing the project is small

313

(3 to 6 weeks, several months) "waterfall" projects. The result of each project should be something that can be delivered to the stakeholders of the project.

At first this will be a prototype (if you're lucky) and a something that looks as a business model.
After a few iterations, after baselining the architecture and at least one architecture prototype, you start by implementing the core functionality of your system.

Gradually you extend (if you have the time) iteration per iteration more and more functionality.
I say "if you have the time" since "timeboxmanagement" is quite important. Even if not all requirements are implemented, you have to deliver and learn from the process.
This is what iteration is all about, learning from the past and formalizing that knowledge in the process.

So in fact an iterative process is based on one or more "waterfall" processes. The waterfall process is NOT bad, the iterative approach is simply something extra.
In a way the iterative approach is related with Component Based Development where you also start from "core" functionality and gradually move towards more specialized functionality.

Question 95: *Project management resources*

I am looking to enhance my project management skills. Does anyone have any good books, sites, schools or even certifications that may help?

A1: The best that I have found have been:

1) Software Project Survival Guide
2) Code Complete
3) Debugging the software Development Process

All are from Microsoft Press.

You might want to look at Project Management Institute (PMI)
But I think they are a little to complicated for the average Software Dev. Group.

A2: Please check out the SEI and other answers to my similar question above. The PMI has an IS Special Interest Group also, I am just joining it now so will see what they have to offer. Although the PMI seems widely known for project management, a lot of their material relates to non-IS project management, but I'm going to go ahead and get that certificate anyway, as it is much less expensive than SEI courses, so easier to get management to pay for. SEI is specifically oriented to Software acquisition or development, and how to build an organization that supports that. Note for PMI Cert you have to have several years of project management experience before they allow you to take the test, but you can join the organization with no experience. Local chapters offer training for the cert test and the national conferences have prep sessions available too.

A3: I first must clarify that we are talking about traditional project management.
There are inherent errors and problems with the traditional approach. It is one reason why 80% of all projects fail to meet scope, cost, or schedule. I'll cover the new approach later.

A very good book, recommended by PMI is Effective Project Management -second edition, by Robert K Wysocki, Robert beck Jr., David B, Crane, it comes with a CD.
Wiley is the publisher. It's excellent.
Then there is the good old Project Management for Dummies, the 1st to read if you have been away too long from it. And/Or the Idiots guide to Project Management. I'm not making fun of you I have them both myself.
There's a very thin book, not quite 1/2 an inch called Fundamentals of Project Management by James P Lewis. It covers a lot in a very clear manner.
Then I have used Project Management for the 21st Century, by Bennet P Lientz and Kathryn P. Rea.

Another that helps a lot but is not strictly PM is Dr James C Wetherbe's and Nicholas P. Vitalari's book "Systems Analysis and Design - Best Practices" it covers do a good requirements statement and other parts of PM.

Now you can find the Little Black Book of Project Management, and big thick books, I find they all are covering the same ground. I believe these would prepare you for a sizable project.

Now a better way to conduct and manage projects takes a lot of learning, so I can't teach it here but I can point you to the path. It is the way projects are done within the body of Knowledge call the "Theory of Constraints". The specific project method is called CCPM Critical Chain Project Management. You must learn the Theory of Constraints for learning CCPM. It is a serious departure from the traditions PM method so you must for now jus continue with that. But I tell you so you know the truth and can learn. If you search the web with that phase you will find a world you may never knew existed.

Question 96: Project Teams and Leadership

I am currently in my fourth year of a Software Engineering degree and I have
to deliver a presentation for Software Project Management on the following:

Many programmers view group development & team building with skepticism. They were selected for their programming skills, not their social skills, for coding more than cooperation.

I am just looking for a few points of view from people that are involved in project management so I can compare my feelings and opinions regarding project teamwork.

How important is teamwork in delivering a project on time and within cost?

A: A good team is more than the sum of the individuals, a good and motivated team can beat all odds (easy and open communication).

However, you cannot "force" people into teamwork. If there is mutual respect and of being open is rewarded, then the stuff comes naturally.

Teamwork is not a goal on its own. The lone wolf developer that programs alone at night can be highly productive and valuable for the project team, without being physically in the team.

It is the role of the project manager to manage all the individuals into the right balance and mix.

Question 97: Vanilla Method

I have been hearing a lot during business meetings about "Vanilla method".

What does this means?

A1: Vanilla usually means "Without frills" such as "plain Vanilla". Like going out for ice cream and they ask you do you want syrup, nuts, cherries, etc. No just "plain vanilla". As in the simple solution, or the obvious solution.

A2: In this case, your "basic PMing" is going to consists of the simple things: Time, Scope, Cost management... To Eyeswideclosed's comment, this is certainly a point where someone is either wants to be ambiguous, thus placing the responsibility on you for everything, so if they don't get something they want, they will come back and say, "Well, we told you very clearly we wanted "X" level of service". Be very careful about that. As a PM the best thing you can do is to create either a Project Definition Report, or a Project Execution Plan that clearly defines the deliverables, when they will be delivered, and who is responsible for their creation.

That way, you have something to come back to if they try to blow the scope of your activities suddenly deciding that you are responsible for managing the P/L when in reality you should just be tracking project expenses to the budget they have laid out.

Just an example... but yes, when I hear a term like that used in a meeting to describe what I will be doing, it sends of big red flags...

Question 98: Managing external partners

I have had a couple of encounters with external partners with which we have been working on projects for exchanging data. Let me briefly try to explain what's happened.

After setting the specifications about the data to be exchanged, both ends (we and the external partner) build our own software to exchange the data (different systems required different software - we don't have any insight in the external partner's system, and they have no insight in our system, so we have both done the work needed on our own end).

During testing problems popped up - some bugs that needed to be fixed (no problems with that), but what has been troubling me are the issues where the external partner had "changed" the specifications about the protocol, without consulting or informing us: sending different data than agreed upon in the specs.

The question I am struggling with is how to get the external partner to adhere to the specifications? I have just referred to the specs, but the external partner is a rather large organization, and we are much smaller. Arguments like, "we have put so much effort and money in this exchange" are given to explain their changes and their unwillingness to revert to the specs, but none of these arguments cut any wood...

I disagree with the change at this stage of the project and would not want to change to software on our end just because they are not adhering to the specs...

So, how would you handle such a situation? How can I

convince the external partner to stick with the original plan and specs? How can I manage external partners?

A: Well first of all, this is NOT typical for one particular sector, so don't worry.

The main concern for me would be who's paying and responsible for the overall progress? Typically if there is a single customer giving two third parties the job to integrate two systems, the proper way is to let them decide. A typical response from me would be to the customer:

"He, we have a change in specs. Fine by me, but that will cost an extra X bucks. And BTW it will add an additional risk to the deadline and stability of the interface. Could you please sign off the request for change?"

And if they respond "No way are you mad!?" just indicate to tell the other supplier to stick to the plan.

So, who is picking up the tab, has the responsibility and, of course, what were the original agreements.

Question 99: Moving to .net framework

The company I am working for has developed an application, which has been deployed at many offices of many clients, about 700. For the last 10 years now we want to move to .net framework. The core functionality needs to remain the same but we want ease of deployment (so thinking of smart client), cleaner and flexible program (present software has many bugs and is rigid). Now my concern is that the existing database design is not optimized as per normalization rules and we would like to redesign it which means the data in the existing databases will need to be ported. What are the various ways one can go about it? Good practices? Or other option is to with present database only and just develop the application.

How big a risk this will be?

A1: It is rather difficult to say... is the current database structure causing any problems? Performance, maintainability, etc. how much do these problems costs you and your customers?

If you want to change to a different db design, will it solve the problems? Will it introduce new ones? Do your customers want this? Who will pay for all data migrations? Is it worth it?

If you need to change the structure, it seems the time is now when you are rebuilding your system completely anyway.

Question remains: is the change needed because "it needs to be normalized" or is the current design causing problems?

A2: As the time passes by its better to move on from legacy systems. .net is a great choice but before starting with new systems it's wise to analyze the problems and new features that may make the software with tune to the time.

.Net offers great advancements and its better to have application architecture in place before proceeding.

Question 100: Project Failure

Why does a project fail?

A: June 07, 2006 (Computerworld) -- SCOTTSDALE, Ariz. -- Failing to initiate "crucial conversations" may be the single biggest cause of project failure, according to preliminary findings of an ongoing study on project management.

The study, being conducted by Vital Smarts Inc., a Provo, Utah-based training firm, found that project managers' inability to talk to people about five often-occurring negative situations frequently leads to failure. The preliminary findings were made public here yesterday at Delivering Project Excellence, a conference for project managers.

According to David Maxfield, director of research at Vital Smarts, the five situations include the following:

Setting arbitrary deadlines and inadequate resources that "set up a project to fail."

Failing to provide the necessary leadership, political clout or energy for a project.

Skirting or manipulating the project priority-setting process.

An unwillingness by team members to support projects as required.

Failing to acknowledge project problems until it's too late for remedial action.

About 150 project managers in the audience supported the findings with numerous comments and a show of hands, indicating that they confront such situations regularly.

Maxfield reported that surveys and interviews of more than 800 project managers, as well as 150 hours of observations of corporate project activities, indicated that 80% of project managers routinely face arbitrary deadlines and inadequate resources that have no relationship to reality and only 18% who feel they can confront that situation effectively.

Maxfield pointed to the key difference between those who don't confront arbitrary deadlines and those who do: Those who don't "think of all the bad things that will happen if they stand up to their boss," he said. Those who do talk about their concerns "think of all the bad things that will happen if they don't stand up."

When such crucial conversations don't occur, he said, projects suffer. According to Maxfield, 74% come in over budget, 82% miss deadlines, 79% fail to meet quality or functional specifications, and 67% result in damaged team morale.

A comprehensive report on the data will be released in September, but Maxfield said preliminary results indicate an overwhelming need for project managers to "speak truth to power" as well as for corporate leaders to make it safe for that to happen.

Leaders, he said, need to create a culture where crucial conversations are consistently held, and they must measure their progress in creating such a culture as a leading indicator of project success.

Meanwhile, individual project managers can make an immediate difference by increasing their competence at initiating and holding these crucial conversations, Maxfield said. "When you speak up, you make it safer for everyone around you to speak up; and when you don't speak up, you make it harder for everyone around you to speak up," he said.

Because these situations tend to reflect patterns of process violations, he said, project managers who can confront and resolve them "get incredible leverage for improvement."

Acronyms:

WBS	-	Work Breakdown Structure
UML	-	Unified Modeling Language
RUP	-	Rational Unified Process
SDP	-	Streaming Download Project
PMI	-	Project Management Institute
SCM	-	Software Configuration Management
DSS	-	Defense Security Service

INDEX